The
Return

Also by J. John with Chris Walley

The Life: A Portrait of Jesus

The Return
Grace and the Prodigal

J.JOHN
WITH
CHRIS WALLEY

HODDER &
STOUGHTON

First published in Great Britain in 2010 by Hodder & Stoughton
An Hachette UK company

1

A CIP catalogue record for this title is available from the British Library

ISBN 978 0 340 99514 3
Trade Paperback ISBN 978 0 340 99515 0

Typeset in Garamond by Ellipsis Books Limited, Glasgow

Printed and bound by Clays Ltd, St Ives plc

Hodder & Stoughton policy is to use papers that are natural,
renewable and recyclable products and made from wood grown
in sustainable forests. The logging and manufacturing processes
are expected to conform to the environmental regulations
of the country of origin.

Hodder & Stoughton Ltd
338 Euston Road
London NW1 3BH

www.hodderfaith.com

Contents

CONTENTS

General Introduction

This book is an exploration of a story that has two claims to greatness. The first claim is that it is a perfect story: brief, flawlessly crafted and with three characters with whom we can all identify. The second is that it is about the most important of matters – how God relates to human beings – from the most authoritative source on such issues. The story is commonly called 'The Prodigal Son' and although it isn't the best title ('The Father and his Two Sons' might be better), we will use the traditional term for it throughout.

The book is divided into three parts. In the first part there is what we might call a reimagining of the story of the Prodigal Son. We have expanded it and moved it into a setting that is probably a little easier to identify with. Our reasons for doing this will become clear; let's just say here that sometimes familiarity brings not so much contempt as complacency, and that is just as dangerous. By giving the story a makeover, we hope it has regained something of the drama to surprise in our culture that the original had in its day. In the second part we look at Jesus' original story, examine it in detail and tease out what it has to say to us about God. In the third part we try to apply the message of the parable of the Prodigal Son to our own lives.

There are two things to say right at the start about the authorship of this book. The first is that this is a collaboration. J.John is a preacher, speaker and canon in the Anglican Church, while Chris Walley is a teacher, writer, geologist and an elder and preacher in a Baptist church. We have worked together a number of times before, most notably on *The Life: A Portrait of Jesus*. You may wish to play the game of asking yourself 'Who wrote which bit?' but it's a waste of time: it really is a collaboration. The second thing – and it's an important one – is that in a sense neither of us is a typical Western teacher/preacher. J.John spent his early years in Cyprus, whose culture is not a million miles removed from that of the Bible, and speaks the modernised form of the Greek of the New Testament. Chris spent eight years of his life lecturing at the American University of Beirut, teaching, amongst others, students from villages in Lebanon where the lifestyle and values have changed little in two thousand years. We have drawn on these backgrounds not just in the story of the Salvadori family that begins the book, but throughout.

Two more things. First, we are both in various ways communicators, and together we have sought to make this an engaging book. We have not, however, sought liveliness at the expense of truth; we have struggled with commentators and translations and have tried to make sure that any conclusions we have made are justified. (As we did with *The Life*, we have, for the most part, put Bible references and suggestions for further reading at the back of the book, while using footnotes for minor observations.) Second, in writing on this most discussed parable it would be all too easy to create little more than a compilation of what has already been said. We have made it a point to try to be fresh. In the presence of the brilliance of the story of the Prodigal Son, showing a little bit of originality is the least we can do.

PART ONE

The Road Home

PERSONAE

Francis Nutrizio, steward and narrator
Theodore Salvadori, master of the Salvadori estate
Katerina Salvadori, his wife
Andreas Salvadori, their elder son
Yiannis Salvadori, their younger son
Despina Aristophanes, lady-in-waiting

1

Five short, blunt words. Beating at the door, ringing in my ears, shouting at the window on a dark, clear night; driving me to God-knows-where, to a place I might have glimpsed but not yet seen; bereft of grid reference or signpost.

Which way do we go?

The future is an empty horizon. The past slips away like the wake of a boat sailing to the edge of the known world. Soon I will be gone. Yet in the turmoil of a world turned upside down, a still, sacred moment of presence offers itself as a lifeline. In the eye of the hurricane, it can suddenly seem eerily still. And in this deepest of nights, in the stillness of a moment held captive, one simple question demands an answer before time is released once more and day breaks like a wave on the rest of my days.

Which way do we go?

My name is Francis Nutrizio. For most of my life I have kept a meticulous record of my master's business. Now it is time to tell of my own. And I have just one night to do so: huddled at this old, familiar friend of a table, wrapped in a blanket against the cold and searching for words by the light of a single flame. Although it is late, sleep can wait like a dog outside the door. For who cares if I am tired tomorrow? After twenty years, it is my last day as steward to the Salvadori family of High Florent.

First, I must explain how I came to be in this position as steward to the House of Salvadori, serving the good Lord Theodore and his two sons. My own family are not of this region; the House of

Nutrizio is noble enough in the west of our country, and I will never know what made my grandparents move far to the east. But whatever it was, it was not a wise move. The result was a life of poverty, for both themselves and their children. My parents, despite their terrible fortune, retained their dignity and were fiercely ambitious – if not for themselves, then at least for me. From the earliest age, they drove it into me: work hard and make a good name for the family and myself. Reputation mattered. *Our* reputation mattered.

When I was barely thirteen, hell came calling. It was a winter's night and a candle was left carelessly alight as we slept. My father had probably drunk a dram too much spirit to warm his soul. But warm him it did. I thought I was dreaming of the lake of fire until I awoke to blood-red flames raging through our house. Miraculously someone, somehow, saved me (to this day I know not who); my parents never even made it out of their room.

An aunt took care of me. She was kind, if not adoring. She did ensure that my education continued and four years later, when I reached seventeen, life took a turn – the kind that you hardly notice at the time but, on looking back, you can see quite clearly that it was a fork in the road. This was my turning point: I had the good fortune to join the Salvadori family in the upper part of the Florent Valley. As the estate is remote, the family is renowned for recruiting orphans who do not need to spend days away visiting their families. Upon my arrival as a fresh-faced young man eager to impress, I set to work: first as a junior clerk in the steward's office – the kingdom of the unforgettable Marco. Marco was a thick-set man whose eyebrows joined at the centre and who, whatever the weather, dressed like a raven in thick black robes. He always laughed from the depth of his belly, especially after three or so jars of his favourite dark ale with the locals from the town; yet for all his merriment, he was widely feared. Marco knew everything and everyone, and he knew exactly how to get what he wanted from them.

My apprenticeship with Marco, however, was the opportunity of a lifetime and only a fool would not have seized it with both hands. I worked harder than a donkey, finding out how every aspect of the estate worked. My father, and later my aunt, had taught me never to accept bribes – for this was dishonourable – and soon my reputation as a trustworthy man spread. Over the next two years I learned my business inside out – the jobs that needed to be done, and how, so that the estate would run smoothly and efficiently. I soon knew which tenant farmers we could trust to pay us on time and which would need one of Marco's dreaded 'visits'. And I learned the challenges of each different season: to repair the cisterns before the rains of winter; to hire men before the ploughing season; to stock up with wood before the snows made the high forest inaccessible to our horses and mules.

Marco began to entrust me with more and more. And why not? It made life easier for him. Soon I was supervising the shepherds' accounts – a difficult task, because they are unreliable and untrustworthy (and who knows how many sheep a shepherd really has?). But I succeeded in my task, and within another eighteen months I was running the tenant farmers' accounts. By my twentieth birthday, I was accompanying Marco to meet with the Lord Theodore himself. It was an incredible privilege, but a daunting task. The first time I entered his rooms, I was concentrating so hard that I almost tripped and fell headlong into a chambermaid. Gradually I found that I need not worry. My Lord Theodore was a kind man and sympathetic to my nervous stuttering (although he only asked who I was, and how I was, and whether I had learned to count properly at school, unlike the tax collectors . . .). In time I found that the rumours were true: Theodore and his wife, the Lady Katerina, disliked Marco but had come to find him indispensable. I also learned another lesson: that the good steward has little to fear – only the most foolish of masters gets rid of a competent steward.

Just after my twenty-first birthday, Marco grew ill and I found myself taking on more responsibility. No one quite knew what was ailing him, but on a cold spring day when the winds blew across the mountain and rattled at the shutters, Marco winced with pain, clutched at his heart and toppled from his chair. He lay on the floor, a great, charcoal mound that heaved, and then fell still. The raven was gone without so much as a goodbye. I was immediately appointed acting steward and in the following weeks my Lord looked for a replacement, but no one more suitable could be found. Of course, there were those who said it was wrong and too big a risk to leave someone so young to manage the accounts. Still, the Lord Theodore, who had little time for honour or shame, over-ruled the objections. So there it was: at the age of twenty-two I became steward at this beautiful estate.

Although I did not know it, in the twenty years since I joined, I would witness the household at its greatest time. Our estate was one of the largest in the Prince's realm. It was like a great, wide spoon of land that straddled the River Florent as it flowed down from the mountains of the north to the great rocky gorge in the south. While much of it was flat meadowland by the river, it also ran up either side to the high foothills of the mountains. If you were to ride the borders of the estate – and I often did just that, especially in summer at sunset, when the light made the river shine like liquid gold – it would take three days. In the upper reaches, we would have to dismount and walk through the dark woods and mountain pastures. Sheep grazed the pastures, and the woods yielded timber for building and firewood to keep us warm in winter. On the descent, you passed through terraced slopes rich with fruit orchards, olive trees and vineyards. Towards the Florent, the land gently eased into meadows for cows, fields full of wheat and ponds for fish. A number of springs bubbled to the surface there, few of which failed even in the driest years. The land was kind to us.

In fact, we had everything we needed. My Lord Theodore once

turned to me and, with a smile of contentment, declared, 'Francis, this is not just an estate; it is a world.' He was right. Had pestilence or war sealed us off, we could have lived well enough on what we had in the valley alone. As it was, we traded profitably with the towns and cities below us. The house lay at the heart of the estate. It stood proudly on a mound, a broad, graceful building supported by columns and crowned with a terracotta roof. I have seen other great houses and many of them were adorned with towers, battlements and high walls. The great house of Salvadori was different: it was, as someone said (using the old Latin word), a villa. It was surrounded not by high ramparts but by low walls, by gardens and hedges. It was open in both appearance and spirit. It boasted a lofty timbered hall with balconies and a great fireplace which kept it warm in winter when the winds blew off the icy mountaintops. A stone's throw away, and separated by a pencil line of poplars, stood the offices, stables, workshops and servants' quarters. And scattered around the house and the offices were nearly two hundred cottages – for those who depended on the estate.

An estate, however, is not just the land and its crops; it is the family. I began to serve the Salvadori household when the Lord Theodore was in his forties; he was tall and well built and moved with impressively youthful energy. I came to know and love him well and, as I write, I grieve his passing, which is fresh. Theodore was an intelligent, thoughtful and compassionate man. I might have added 'pious', but Theodore had little time for the religious leaders of the town and their banal rituals and was, by all accounts, considered by them to be irreligious or worse. Yet in private he was a man of faith and reverence, a thoughtful reader of the Holy Scriptures. He cared for his people and they, on the whole, cared for him. He gave them work, enforced laws, built schools and provided a doctor, and was the willing and generous sponsor of celebrations and festivals.

Theodore ruled the estate with wisdom and grace. Yet he was

a reluctant leader; he had been the younger of two sons and it was only his brother's tragic death from a hunting fall that made him heir. When, in due course, his father died, he was obliged to take on the estate out of a sense of duty. At times he must have wished he could escape from this role and the burdens of management. Once, as we drank a glass of wine together after another long day, he confided in me that as a youth he wanted to leave the valley and travel to see the wide world beyond. As he spoke, he stared out at the road south and I caught a wistful yearning in his face.

Perhaps his reluctance to take the job explained his occasional insensitivity to the demands of honour and decency. He was a man who was irritated by the constraints that tradition and duty place on us all. This disrespect for tradition was clear even in simple things, such as the way he carried himself. Everyone knows how a ruler of any sort, even the master of a large estate, should move: slowly, solemnly, with decorum and dignity and always without haste; he should never perspire or look flushed, urgent or hasty. To do so is to lose dignity, or, as we say here, to lose face. But Theodore did not seem to care; he never possessed what the ancients called *gravitas* and cared little for the manner and style of power and position. Here is as good a place as any to record my only complaint of him: that his generosity of spirit would often undermine my own position and authority. I valued kindness as much as anyone, but as the head of an estate, resolve and unwavering firmness are vital. Each autumn I would work through a list of our tenant farmers, draft their bills and dispatch them. But within days I would inevitably find myself summoned to meet Theodore in his study, which was piled high with books and furnished only with two simple chairs and a battered table. There, standing on the threadbare carpet, I would see another teary peasant clutching their bill. Inevitably, Theodore would tell me how his heart had been touched by the unprecedented plight of this particular farmer and how – if I concurred – he would like the sum to be reduced or payment postponed. Of course, I had no option but to bow my head and acknowledge his wisdom and generosity. He did not do it too frequently (and no one ever got away with it more than once or twice), but still, it undermined my authority. The wise ruler runs his estate well by strengthening, not weakening, his steward's authority.

Of the Lady Katerina, I have fewer memories, for she died over ten years ago. But I cherish those memories I do have, of a small woman who was merry and carefree. When I visited the house I would often hear her singing. Strangely, Theodore treated her as an equal partner, something unheard of in our land, almost shocking and, many believe, dishonourable. After all, in our world it is deemed right that, while women are to be treated with honour and praise, they are also to keep silent and it is best for them to stick to their own concerns. But Theodore would have none of that. Sometimes he would invite me into the main room where the Lady Katerina would witness our deliberations, quietly sewing or making some tapestry – but listening to every word. Often, Theodore would pause in his conversation with me and turn to ask for her opinion. It was, I thought, quite odd, but this *equality* that he granted her also hinted at what was to come in his relationship with his two sons. But I jump ahead of myself.

My master and the estate remained at the centre of things. Every month, the lords of the adjacent lands – the Mouzakis from the west, the Tavionos from the east, the Carreris from the south – and sometimes others would ride up with their carriages and finest horses to visit. My Lord would hold court in the villa. It was a fine gathering of nobles and the honour that they paid to my master was gratifying: he was held up as their head and his advice was sought and taken. The lords would gather around a long table and after wine and mezes there would be much discussion of important matters.

I felt privileged to be there, seated behind my master. Frequently in the discussions he would tilt his head back towards me, I would lean forward and he would whisper to me questions such as 'How much does the House of Tavionos owe us?' or 'How much are we getting for figs and olives these days?' and I would whisper back the answer. He would nod and, armed with the facts, turn back to the discussion. I watched closely at these meetings and listened with the greatest care, preparing myself for those moments when my master would need my knowledge. Seated there, slightly in the shadows, I could keep a close eye on things. My Lord Theodore was certainly respected – people rose when he entered, kissed his hand and smiled at his humour. He came from a distinguished line and our estate was the most prestigious around. But this respect was tinged with a darker edge; behind the bows and careful words, I noted carefully how they all watched him. There were those who would have liked to buy land from him, others hankered after more generous contracts with our estate, and some were deeply envious of his position.

Once a year in May, my Lord Theodore and I would ride to the city, where he and I would meet with the Prince's managers to discuss and agree the tribute due to the Prince. On the following day, my Lord would meet privately with him and renew his oath of loyalty. Then we would return. The sight of our carriage gliding over the crest of the hill and down the long drag to the town would be the signal for joy and celebrations. They were golden days and it is not just the benefit of hindsight that tells me so. There were threats of war, rebellions and famine, but they all passed by our valley. It was by no means a perfect world, but it was as happy as they come in these imperfect times.

2

Now you know the background, my tale must proceed quickly. The first rays of dawn will soon be scoring the darkness, when I must be away.

Within a year of my arrival, Lady Katerina became pregnant and the first son was born on a warm, late spring evening when the storks were flapping northwards overhead. They called him Andreas. We spin our children the familiar yarn that storks bring babies, and with Andreas it was easy to believe. Three years later, a second son was born in midsummer and he was named Yiannis. Theodore's happiness seemed to be complete. He had two sons and the future of his family appeared to be secure.

Yiannis was one year old when I was made steward and I came, of course, to know him and his brother well. It is easy, looking back, to trace the seeds sown of what was later to come; the boys were always so different from each other. However far back I stretch for my recollections of Andreas, I always remember him as a solemn, thoughtful and watching child. Yiannis was different: lighter in complexion and manner, a carefree, relaxed boy who wanted to explore everything. It was easy to like 'Yianni', as he came to be called by many. I refused to use this shorter name myself; it would not have been proper. It was a mark of the difference between the two that Andreas similarly would not allow any abbreviation of his name.

As they grew up, both boys would visit my office. Andreas would stand alongside me, look at the accounts and ask what I was doing.

Sometimes I would let him play with the bright counters and he would sit and make columns with them before returning them in neat piles. Yiannis would also come, but if it were the counters that attracted his attention, he would help himself and scatter them in a mess upon the floor. When he grew bored and wandered away, I would have to retrieve them – on my hands and knees – from the four corners of the office. Yiannis, however, soon acquired an interest in reading books, and from an early age was often to be found in the library reading fiction, tales of far-distant places and of traditions other than our own. As he grew, he would leave the house and wander through the town. Of course my master was so highly respected that he never came to harm and sooner or later a workman would carry him back on his mule or over his shoulder, to be rewarded with a few shiny coins from Theodore. Occasionally Yiannis would climb the watchtower by the stable and gaze out into the distance, down the dusty road that ran up the grey hills and out of the valley.

Although Yiannis's free spirit made him an attractive child, from a very early age he showed signs of disrespect. He would saunter into my office, even when I was busy in negotiations, and tug at my coat, demanding, yes *demanding*, that I give him some counters or some paper to write on. Of course, as he was my master's son, I granted his requests, but it was not proper. I could see the amusement written on the faces of those I was trying to deal with and felt shamed. I could recall many similar instances. There were some who said that his father should have disciplined Yiannis earlier and more severely, but it is not the task of a steward to judge how his master runs his family.

The two boys never really got on with each other. They were, by temperament, like chalk and cheese. I found I liked Yiannis but did not respect him and, while I respected Andreas, I couldn't warm to him.

As the boys grew, so did my role. Theodore came to put the

highest trust in me. I rode with him everywhere and he and I came to be as close as a steward and master could be. In fact, he seemed like a father. The weather was kind to us in those years; the crops flourished, the estate prospered and all was well. In my fifth year as steward, the Prince himself visited us and stayed for three days. I had never faced a greater challenge; my work was unrelenting, but all went well and the Prince left us greatly pleased and lavished my master with praise.

On the great days, the feasts, the Saints' Days, when the flags would fly and the drums and trumpets sounded, I could not help loving this estate and being proud of all that we had come to be.

I had been given the house that Marco had previously filled with his brooding presence. It was too big for me, but I made it comfortable. I lived prudently. Sometimes I considered marriage, but I had found no one suitable; I held to the maxim that a steward's position, midway between his lord and his people, is delicate and he must therefore choose his wife carefully. Sadly, in such a small town, there were few families with whom an alliance would have been appropriate, and those that there were had no eligible daughters. I wondered about finding a girl from the city, but I was there so rarely that I knew few people, and besides, who would have let their daughter go and live with me? So I made the best of my situation and reconciled myself to a life of domestic solitude, which I eased by reading books from my Lord's considerable library. In fact, as I threw myself increasingly into my work, my periods of leisure were few.

As I have said before, when you are wandering down the road of life it can sometimes take a subtle yet significant turn. And so, in my tenth year at the estate, my Lady Katerina acquired a lady-in-waiting, Despina Aristophanes. Despina was from the city and also an orphan, but unlike me from no family of name. I had never heard of the Aristophanes family and neither, it seemed, had anyone else. In fact, I thought she was common and lacked the dignity that servants in such an intimate role ought to have. She seemed a rather strange creature, with long dark hair, a thin face and sharp brown eyes that had a way of looking at everything with an amusement that seemed most improper.

At first, I had little to do with Despina; the only interest a steward has in his Lady's maidservants is their cost to the estate. Increasingly, though, she made her presence felt – and we soon clashed. She had the audacity, having only just arrived and hardly having had time to unpack her things, to come to me with a list of items that she wanted for her room. I stared at her with incredulity, and asked to see the Lady Katerina's signature of approval. She replied with a brazen look that it was what she personally wanted. I explained, as calmly as I could, that this was not how things worked around here. She glared back. 'Steward Francis,' she said, in a voice loud enough for others to hear, 'that may be the way that things worked in the past, but I would like another way. My Lady has granted me authority to make such requests for myself.'

This display of arrogance, from someone ten years my junior and newly arrived to the estate, was maddening. But I bit my tongue and bowed, explaining that I would have to seek clarification and thus postpone any decision. When I consulted with my Lord, he blushed and admitted that his wife had asked for such a privilege and it had been granted. The incident spoke volumes about Despina's attitude and also that of my master – one demanding, the other compromising.

A year after Despina had swept into the household, the Lady Katerina fell pregnant again. How I wish that the storks really did deliver our babies! Childbirth is a dangerous business and thus it was proved, most grievously. We had prepared to throw one of our famous celebrations, yet instead we turned to darkness and mourning. There were 'complications' – a euphemism if ever I heard one, for goodness knows what it was that killed her – and, just like my mother and father, and Marco, our Lady Katerina disappeared from the road of my life without warning. The baby, a girl, died later that day. Perhaps it was just as well. A shadow fell across the whole estate.

Had my Lady Katerina lived, events in the future might have been different.

3

My Lord grieved passionately for his wife. He refused to shave for weeks, and life seemed to drain from his face. He might have been present in body but his spirit was surely elsewhere, searching for his lost companion, shouting from the hills, chasing through the valleys where she loved to walk, but never catching up with her. For months I found myself making decisions on the estate. Then slowly, wearily, reluctantly, Theodore hauled himself back from wherever he had been; dawn began to rise on this long, dark night of the soul, and slowly he began to reassert control. After all, we needed him. And deep down, he needed us.

When the Lady Katerina left us, I expected Despina to go too. She had other plans, however, and stayed firmly put. She took charge of the female workers in the house and, in so doing, undertook a lesser, domestic counterpart to my job. We now met more frequently and I admit that, slowly, I acquired a sneaking respect for her. Anyway, a steward must learn to put his own feelings to one side and I could see that she had competence and honesty. And I saw that she, like me, seemed to find her purpose in service to the Salvadori estate.

Respect is not affection, however, and she still displayed that infuriating disregard for matters of honour which I cannot abide. Her dress and way of speaking were never sufficiently formal for a figure of her position, and she should have taken more care with whom she associated. Once, as I rode past the market, I saw her down in the stalls shopping and she was laughing and joking with the merchants. She saw me and didn't even have the humility to look chastened. I think this was partly her upbringing, but I felt that it was something Theodore had encouraged by his reluctance to impose his will on her in such matters. They were, it would seem, kindred spirits.

For the purpose of my tale, I can skip through those years. It became clear to anyone who had eyes to see that trouble would arise with the children. On the face of it, Andreas was the model son: hard-working, diligent, aware of his destiny, forever riding around the estate and watching the proceedings with a stern eye. He took to giving orders to the people and although at first this seemed amusing, as he grew up it became irritating and presumptuous. It undercut both my authority and that of his father and eventually we issued a ruling that while Master Andreas was to be honoured, all orders were to come only through myself or from the Lord Theodore.

Yiannis, however, gave the greatest cause for concern with his many escapades. On one occasion, for instance, while in his early teens, he wandered into the drinking house during a night of peasant dancing and I had to rescue him from under a table where, after too much to drink, he had fallen asleep. Another time he vanished overnight and we later discovered that he had spent the night under the stars, as if he were a tramp. In each case, Theodore frowned and had angry words to say – but nothing more. And in each case, after a brief respite, the tension would surface again.

By the time I reached my twenty-first year with the estate, Yiannis was eighteen and, from what I could see, craved freedom. He argued regularly with his father, though I did not pay the fall-outs too much attention as they did not involve me. However, one April evening while I was working late in my office, the door opened and in walked my Lord Theodore. I rose to my feet and bowed; he closed the door behind him, took a seat and sighed. It was not unusual for my Lord to consult with me, but normally he asked for me to come to him. It is the way such things are done.

'May I talk with you?' he asked quietly.

'Of course, my Lord,' I replied, surprised at his tone and concerned by the troubled look on his face.

He hesitated, leaned forward towards my desk and started fiddling with some pencils. 'I have a difficult problem to resolve,' he said in a slow, strained tone. 'I would like your advice.'

He looked up at me with sad eyes.

'Of course, Sir,' I replied. 'I understand that you are often given difficult questions to resolve.'

'Quite so. It is a delicate case. A younger son wants to take his inheritance in a sizeable estate and leave.'

I stared at him, but he seemed to avoid my gaze.

'My Lord, that is unusual but not a real problem. After the death of the father, an estate is divided and it is our tradition that the elder has two-thirds, the younger has a third. Normally both would keep their property. But, in theory, the younger could do as he wished. I do not see a problem.' I was rather tired and wondered why he had bothered me with such a straightforward case.

'There is a problem. The father is not yet dead.'

'You mean . . .' I paused, trying to get my mind around the appalling case. 'The son – the younger son – wishes to sell what would be his before his father dies?' I was aware of the tone of incredulity in my voice.

He nodded.

'That would be extraordinary. No, *unforgivable*!' Theodore raised an eyebrow, and I continued. 'To ask for an inheritance before a father dies would be an insult of the highest order. It is equivalent to saying to one's father, "I wish you were dead." The family in which it happened would be subject to the deepest shame.'

Theodore's face paled and a bell of warning sounded in my

mind. Surely not, I thought in sudden alarm; he cannot possibly be referring to Yiannis.

'Nevertheless,' Theodore said, in a weary, dogged way, 'suppose that the younger son wished it. Should the father allow it?'

I could see, now, that Theodore was not adjudicating for others. He was agonising over the situation with his own son. I felt my jaw drop and saw him catch my expression. He flushed with shame. I didn't know what to say. It was all I could do not to stutter. 'My honoured and respected Lord, the wisdom of our lands and of our traditions is that such a request should be refused. Indeed, Sir, it is such a dishonourable and shameful request that I have to – reluctantly – say that tradition demands that the child be beaten for even making it.'

I stumbled on. 'Sir, such a request undermines the way we live. It shows disrespect to the family system. It breaks with honour, and honour, as you know, is the cement that holds together the building of our society. To allow for such a decision would be to encourage other similar acts.'

He said nothing, but kept fiddling with those awful pencils. The implications were flooding in now, all of them serious. 'My Lord, for a man to allow such an insult to go unpunished would be to approve of it. It would be badly viewed by both his subjects and his neighbours for similar reasons.' I caught my breath. 'Furthermore, this is not simply a case of blind tradition. Were this landowner to fall ill, it would be the duty of his sons to look after him. And if the inheritance has been squandered, how can he be cared for? Were it to happen, such a man might find that in his old age he was reduced to begging.'

'Indeed.' The single word was all he said.

Silence descended, but it was so awkward that I had to fill it. 'And to sell ancestral lands is neither right nor honourable. We and the land are linked . . .'

'So,' he spoke, looking at me, into me, through me, with his stone-grey eyes. 'You would not advise that such a request be granted?'

Self-preservation began to take over. 'Sir, I am a steward. The job of a steward is to advise on the wise running of an estate. I could not, in all honesty, support such a decision.'

He sighed. 'Francis, I value you enormously and I value your honesty and wisdom. You know, of course, that the one I speak of is Yiannis.' I will not forget the moment as long as I live.

'My Lord, I had wished that it was not so.'

He cleared his throat. 'Were the request to be granted . . . could it be done?'

'It would damage the estate. A third?' I shook my head. 'The best you could do would be to surrender to him the eastern high pastures; the Sefarians would gladly buy that patch.'

Without a word, he rose and went to the open window. He breathed in and stared east towards the pastures that glowed red with the setting sun.

'Sir,' I asked, 'what would he do with the money?'

'I do not know, Francis. He talks about travelling. He is a restless young man. I sympathise with him. I was once like him.'

I hesitated, but felt I had to say more. 'Sir, you have shared your confidence with me and I ask in turn the right to speak freely. I would urge you please to consider any decision gravely. It would damage your estate, your future and your reputation. It cannot even be said, with certainty, that it would be for the good of the young man.'

My words were audacious; for a steward to tell a master how to treat his son is to cross a well-marked boundary. But thankfully this was no ordinary master. 'Francis, you are right. But life and love mean taking risks. And to let him go will hurt me enormously.'

He walked to the door. 'But thank you for your honest advice. It is a father's dilemma.' He sighed. 'If only Katerina were here to advise me.' And with that, he was gone.

I wasted no time in arranging a secret meeting with Despina. Faced with a crisis of such magnitude, it was time to ignore any reservations about the way she handled things. She had heard the rumour and, to her credit, was also perturbed.

'Miss Despina, surely it cannot be allowed? The implications for the estate are appalling. His name would suffer shame.' She stared at me with searching brown eyes – I had never noticed how brown before – and she shook her head. 'Sometimes, Francis, I wonder whether you understand him.'

'How do you mean?'

She clasped her hands together, held them up to her face and stared thoughtfully at me over them. 'Francis, you live for honour, for the name of a thing. He sees that it is the thing itself that matters.'

I felt myself frown.

'He is faced,' she continued, 'with a terrible choice. Either to let Yiannis go free, or to keep him in the valley. If he does the one, he puts his son in a cage. If he does the other, then his son may yet learn to fly.'

I found it hard to read her expression.

'But Miss Despina, if he lets his son go, he will lose him.'

'And Mr Francis,' she replied, teasing me for the formality of my titles, 'if he tries to keep him, he will most certainly lose him.' For a woman who was not a mother, she was disarmingly wise.

'But the estate will suffer.'

She smiled. 'At least we are no longer talking about honour. Yes, it will suffer and your job is to do what you can to minimise such losses.'

'I see.'

She gave me a mischievous look. 'Yes. If it comes to making a settlement, don't let Yiannis know the details. Don't give him all the money and keep some back in a hidden reserve.'

'Why?'

She was rising from her seat. 'Because, much as I love him, Yiannis is a young fool and I think he'll make a mess of it. And what he doesn't know he has, he can't spend. There may come a time when he will need the money.'

'I see,' I muttered, but she had already left.

4

As we feared, the deal went ahead. It took a month to arrange and the Sefarians agreed, as I expected, to take the eastern high pastures and half the slopes at a reasonable price in gold. A clerk from the city drew up the documents, overcharging us as always. The money was transferred and much but not all of it was placed into an account for Yiannis at the city bank. Yiannis had such little business sense that he didn't even bother to check whether it was all that was due to him.

A few days later, Hendrik, the ex-soldier who manages the watch and the patrol of our boundaries, told me that the Sefarians had been moving flocks into the pastures. The man lacks subtlety of any kind and clearly didn't approve as he muttered and spluttered his words of criticism, shaking his head bitterly with resignation. Although I would not voice it, I felt the same. These things, though, were the easier parts of the affair. It was the gossip in town, the widening of eyes, the shaking of heads and the wagging of tongues that was simply unbearable. We were collectively dishonoured. Not only that, but with the transfer of the land, more than ten families lost their livelihoods; they, of course, were furious. And those upholders of our values and standards, the judges and priests, frowned upon the sorry situation and our behaviour.

A week after the deal had been signed, I was tidying my paperwork in the office when there was a furtive knock on my door. It was Yiannis.

I bowed to show him the respect I did not feel.

'I've come to say thank you,' he offered.

'It is my job. My duty is the welfare of the estate.'

'I know you do not approve and I have not come here for your blessing,' he said.

I hesitated before responding. 'Master Yiannis, this will not go down as the greatest event in the history of the Salvadori family.'

Yiannis lifted his head and stared me straight in the eye. He betrayed a look of indignation and pride that I had never seen in his face before. I felt uneasy, but matched his stare. He walked briskly over to my desk, clutched a sheaf of papers and waved them aggressively in my face. 'You live for these things, Francis. I don't.' His voice was hard and passionate. 'I want more than this. I want to be free! To live outside this compound and the rock walls of this valley.'

I froze, as a wave of anger rose within me. What was this talk of freedom? How dare he belittle the world in which his family lived and breathed? And what of our dear Lord Theodore? Hadn't this young man's carefree nature become a selfish lack of regard for anything but his own indulgence? I steadied myself and drew a deep breath. 'Do you care nothing for your home?' I started with a tone more of sadness now than anger. 'What of your father? Do you not love him, Yiannis?'

'I have my own life to live, Francis. I'm leaving tomorrow at dawn.' He spoke his words in a cold, formal voice. I sighed and raised my hand to shake his, but he ignored it. With a stiff nod of his head, he left the room.

The next morning, even before the sun rose, Yiannis slipped away and quiet descended. It was not an easy, proper quiet, however. That he had been allowed to take his inheritance – that he had not been properly disciplined – would have many lasting consequences. Many people were angry with him for being an ungrateful son, of course; but they were livid with Theodore for daring to allow it. The aftershock of this earthquake was felt way beyond its epicentre in the valley. The neighbours did not meet together that month. They all made their excuses: one family had ill health, another had business issues to deal with, still another had an engagement at the Prince's court. Worst of all, in late May, when we journeyed to the city to pay our taxes, Theodore was not granted his usual interview with the Prince. The message was plain: Theodore had undermined everything they stood for and should be punished. Andreas said little, but he had never been talkative. Instead, he scowled. Once, I caught him leaning against the wall of the villa looking towards the eastern heights that no longer belonged to his family, with a face that was purest poison. Although he was glad to see the back of his brother, he plainly disapproved of the decision to sell the land. I rarely saw him talking to his father and, when I did, there was a great deal of strain between them. He was hardened and became increasingly withdrawn, but I still had to respect his ongoing dutiful work for the estate.

And Theodore himself? I'm afraid he made matters worse. There is a time-approved way to treat children who have rebelled. It is harsh but logical: you behave as if they were dead. If he had done so, then things might have been easier, but he didn't. In fact, he did the opposite. He made little secret of his longing for Yiannis to return.

Two months after his son had gone, he summoned me to the villa for a meal. We ate together on the balcony and talked of the estate, but neither Yiannis nor his departure was mentioned. Finally, as the sun dropped over the hills, the bats wheeled above us and the music drifted up from the village, he came to the reason for my visit.

'I was hoping you would do a favour for me.'

'I serve you, my master. Whatever you wish . . .'

'I would like you – quietly – to go down to the city and ask about the whereabouts of a certain young man.'

Inwardly, I groaned; I had hoped that the dreadful matter was buried.

'My Lord, I am willing to do this – but is it wise? What if the Prince gets word? It would bring yet more dishonour to your house.'

'Francis,' his voice became stern. 'I have had enough of the word "honour". I love both my sons and I want Yiannis back. Go to the city and search for him. Go to the port if you don't find him. I have a small portrait you can take. Make copies there.'

I had no choice. Faithful steward that I was, I packed and set off for the capital, ostensibly to see the Prince's managers, but carrying in my saddlebag the portrait of Yiannis and a bag of gold. Once there, I disguised myself as best I could and set about making discreet enquiries. In truth, I hoped I would find the son and persuade him to return. It would be messy, but if he were punished – perhaps made to work in the fields for five years – there might be an end to the whole unhappy episode. But it was not to be.

Instead, matters were worse than I had feared. The story of how my Lord Theodore had let his son go free – disregarding all the rules of honour – was talked of widely in terms of a scandal. I was informed that a news sheet carried an article on the subject, and sermons were being preached in church on the need to punish rebellious sons. I heard these tales, shook my head at them and admitted that the world was in a sorry state for such things to happen.

Finally, after much careful investigation, I learned of a rumour that Yiannis had made for the coast. I rode there – a hard day's journey – and found that he had, indeed, taken a ship across the sea to a distant land in the south. I gave a copy of the portrait to Captain Shakira, who regularly sailed that route and seemed as trustworthy as any seafarer. I left him my address and asked that when he next passed through that port, he make enquiries about Yiannis. A pocketful of gold was the price for his absolute discretion.

I took my time riding back to our valley. The only consolation was that Yiannis was now making a fool of himself in a land so far away that he could drag our name no further into the dirt. Once I was home, Theodore summoned me with unseemly haste. After all my efforts to disguise the nature of my mission, his action seemed so unsubtle that even the dullest servant boy would have guessed what was going on. I conveyed the news I had gathered, and he walked to the window and stared southwards as if, somehow, he could see across the thousand miles or so to where his son was.

'Thank you, Francis,' he said in a low voice. 'Tell me immediately if you hear of anything further.'

It seemed that whenever I visited him through that long summer, he would be standing at the same window, his eyes peering through the heat haze to the shimmering, dusty road below.

I quizzed Despina about how widely she thought word had spread that Theodore was pining for news of his son.

'Everybody knows,' she said, bluntly.

'What happens if he returns?'

'You tell me!' she replied.

'If he's made a fortune, if he comes back in a big gold carriage and throws a big party, he may just get away with it. Success is the only thing that trumps honour.'

'There are other things, Francis . . . but otherwise?'

'It will be a mess.' She nodded and I continued, 'If Theodore handles it properly, we may survive – if he refuses to see him for three days and sentences him to five years' hard labour in the fields, then honour may be satisfied. Justice can sometimes remove shame. But he has brought dishonour in every way on the family estate. He has put people out of work; set a terrible example.'

She gave me one of those looks which made me think she could read my mind. 'Francis, do you really think Theodore will do that? Exact justice?'

'No. But if I hear that Yiannis is on his way back, I will do what I can to make him. The alternatives are far worse.'

She shook her head. 'We'll see.'

For months, no news arrived. And then, as the first snow flurries of autumn had dusted the cloud-wrapped mountain peaks, I received word from the captain. It was a letter which I smuggled to the privacy of my study before opening. I knew that its contents could change our lives for ever.

Dear Steward Francis,

Your friend has made a mess of some business deals. I found him and established that he is the one you seek. He has fallen on hard times. Apparently he earned quite a reputation for himself, throwing his money after wine and women of all sorts. Sons were warned not to trust his word and respectable fathers forbade their daughters to see him. He lived a wild life and has squandered everything. Now he is reduced to taking casual labour of a most unpleasant kind just in order to live; collecting rubbish, working in abattoirs, sleeping rough. I gave him a couple of gold pieces and promised to look out for him again. Knowing that you would reimburse me, I have offered him free passage back any time. But he is a proud soul, even in such dreadful circumstances. Be assured that I am keeping this most confidential.

In your service
Shakira

I headed straight to Despina, who let out a deep groan and agreed it was best that the news be kept from Theodore.

That winter was viciously cold and I found myself glad that at least Yiannis was spared it. As the boats would not sail in winter, I knew that the chances of him returning soon were not good. And, sure enough, there was no further news for months.

Slowly, the thaw came and spring began to speckle the newly green meadows with fresh flowers. Yet the change in season brought no diminution in Theodore's yearning for his son. Inevitably, the person who noticed this more than anyone was Andreas. Once, while looking over the accounts with me, he could contain his bitterness no longer. 'That selfish brother of mine has done enormous damage to our finances. Look at those figures. And still my father longs for his return!' He shook his head angrily. 'The old fool. He should move on!' He spat the words out as if he'd tasted rotten meat. For my part, I maintained a diplomatic silence and continued totalling the figures.

In hindsight, I should have expected the return of Yiannis and I should have talked to Theodore about it beforehand. But hindsight is just that; at the time the matter seemed so difficult that I always managed to put it off. Besides, logic suggested that Yiannis, should he return, would head to the city from where he would send us a humble message asking for reconciliation.

5

It was late April, nearly a year to the day since Yiannis had left, when it happened. I was dictating figures to a clerk when I heard feet pounding across the flagstones to my door. The door was flung open and there was a shout.

'Mr Francis, he's back!'

'*Who's* b–?' I started before working it out for myself.

I jumped up and paced to the door; I wanted to run, but stewards never run. A stable hand had brought me the news and, as I strode past him into the courtyard, there was a great commotion. People were everywhere, mouths agape, whispering and staring, pointing down the road.

My gaze followed their fingers and fell upon the most appalling and dreadful thing I had ever seen. Charging down the steps from the villa and out through the gate, his coat flapping behind him and his feet flying wide in the most undignified manner, was my master. He was *running*. I could have died of shame and embarrassment.

'My Lord!' I cried, but it came out as a squeak as the words choked in my mouth. An under-cook standing next to me began to giggle and I cuffed him, as my turmoil of emotions erupted into anger.

'Get me a horse. *Quick!*' I ordered a gawping groom. 'Get Hendrik,' I yelled, 'and the watch.' I turned to the stable hand, who had followed me out. 'You are sure it's Yiannis?' I still hoped it was a mistake. But he nodded and I saw that he was trying to suppress a grin.

I knew the answer to my next question before I even uttered it. 'Is he wealthy? Has he come with a carriage? On a horse?'

He shook his head. 'He is barefoot. In rags. He has all that he stands up in. No more.'

They brought me a horse, which I mounted with as much dignity as I could muster before clattering down after my master, desperately wondering how we could salvage something, *anything*, of the family reputation.

It was too late. Everyone had taken to the streets of the town. Where had they all come from? The press of bodies was so great that my horse hesitated and halted. I tried to maintain dignity as I was jostled by the crowd, which was swiftly becoming a mob. Ahead I could see my master, still running, the crowd parting in front of him and closing behind him. Then, as he rounded the corner, he came face to face with the skeletal figure of Yiannis, walking with a stick, the ugly, taunting crowd gathering fast and menacingly behind him.

The sight of him took my breath away. No question now that his adventure had been a dismal failure. I shoved through the people urgently, wishing that I had brought a sword. This crowd was angry. I recognised a couple of men who had worked the fields that had been sold; their faces were burning with rage and they clasped stones in their hands.

I was about twenty feet away from Theodore when Yiannis saw his father approaching. For a moment, it felt as though the world had stopped turning. Everything was suspended. Then Yiannis opened his mouth to speak, but could find no words to bring forth. Theodore stumbled towards his son and flung his hands wide, gathering Yiannis into his arms.

I edged nearer. A gruff voice broke the silence, 'Be careful, Mr Nutrizio. Mobs can be funny. You wouldn't want to be caught up in the middle of this one.' I glanced back to see, with relief, Hendrik and some of his biggest men right behind him.

Theodore must have heard Hendrik. Tears running down his ruddy face, his body heaving with exertion and emotion, he turned to us and gasped, 'He is *back*! My son is back!'

Yiannis lifted his sorry head slowly as his eyes met with his father's. As he spoke, his voice cracked with emotion. 'Father, I am sorry. I have done wrong to you. I wish to be treated as less than a servant.'

These words were smothered by a fresh embrace from his father. Then, in a flash, my Lord Theodore lifted his head, looked around at the crowd and raised his shaking voice. 'My friends – *everybody* – the matter is closed.'

The looks of astonishment were writ large on the faces of the crowd. Theodore turned to us. 'A horse for Yiannis, Mr Hendrik. Steward Francis, please return to the house. Have my official robe and my best shoes ready for my son. Have a bath prepared. Summon the doctor.'

I bowed, as much to conceal my confusion as anything else. 'As you wish, my Lord.'

Then he turned to the gawping bystanders and opened his arms wide. 'My son has come home. Tonight, we will have a celebration at the house. Everyone is welcome.' He turned to me, laughter and joy lighting his face. 'Steward, make preparations.'

'*Everyone?*' I coughed.

'Anyone who wants to come.'

How could this be? Where within my Lord Theodore's heart could he find such an ungrudging and spontaneous forgiveness? How could he lavish his love so unsparingly upon this worthless and ungrateful son of his? I knew what I had to do. I stood up in my saddle and waved my hat high. I shouted as loud as I could. 'Three cheers for the Lord Theodore and his son Master Yiannis. Hip, hip . . .'

An appalling silence seemed to stretch out for ever. But then the response came: a great and growing round of hoorays and handclapping stretched through the crowd, and hats were thrown high into the air. I saw two or three stones drop harmlessly to the ground.

As Hendrik and his men dismounted their horses and led them through the crowd, I turned and rode back. Better to play along with this, I thought, stunned by what I had seen. I had served my master for twenty-two years and I wasn't going to betray him now. Besides, whatever my feelings, I needed to back the old man now. A steward must manage any crisis that comes his way. If I kept my composure and handled this well, the name of the House of Salvadori might yet endure.

I rode in through the gate, hurling orders right, left and centre. 'Lunis, unfurl the banners. *All* the banners – every one you can find. Karl, heat the bath water. Matthaeus, summon the doctor. Ah, Phila, get my Lord's best robe ready – the purple one – and some shoes. Do it!'

I drew breath. 'You, get me the cook. Musa, get every employee who isn't dying here in their best clothes within the hour.' And looking around, I shouted: 'Everyone! Master Yiannis is back and the Lord Theodore has been pleased to pardon and restore him. It is a day of rejoicing. If I see anyone who isn't smiling, they are in trouble. I am less forgiving.'

And there, the face I was looking for. 'Despina, a word, please.' I dismounted and we bundled into my office.

'Is it true?' she asked.

'He is back and alive, but barely more.'

'Thank God,' she said, and bowed her head.

'There will be time for that,' I snapped. 'You and I have our greatest challenge.'

'I heard. Theodore has restored him?'

'Totally, publicly. Welcomed him back, announced his restoration.'

She shook her head, and I was sure I could detect the faintest of smiles. 'Extraordinary!'

'I can think of other words for it.'

'You would.'

'My view, Miss Despina, is that he has lost his mind, but that our best hope of salvaging anything from this is to back him.'

She started to say something, but I didn't give her the chance. 'He wants a full-scale banquet with every extravagance lavished upon this feast. Can you do what you can to make it a success?' She closed her eyes and nodded.

'Make sure your ladies sing his praises. Three cheers, that sort of thing. Whatever their private opinions, they are not to show anything other than joy. On pain of dismissal.'

'Very well. There is much to be arranged.' She walked to the door and stopped, her hand resting on the handle.

'Nicely managed, Francis. But can I ask you one question?'

'I have barely time, but yes.'

'Do you care that Yiannis has been found?'

I looked at her blankly, confused. 'No, not really. He was a young fool. He nearly destroyed everything we have worked for. He may do so yet. It might have been better if he had drowned at sea.'

'There is a lot you need to learn,' she replied, looking hurt.

'I'm just doing my business, lady. You do yours.'

She slammed the door behind her and moments later the head cook appeared, his fat face covered in shaving foam and his eyes popping wide open. And so we made our plans and preparations.

6

Somehow we got everything arranged, and by dint of threats, promises and nothing short of bribery on my part, we worked wonders. There was enough meat, wine and bread for the whole town. That, in itself, was enough to put a smile on the faces of those who'd been ready to lynch Yiannis hours earlier. But there was also something strangely uplifting about Theodore's disarming act of reconciliation; it seemed to breed forgiveness in others, too.

People wore their best clothes and all was set for a night to remember. I tried not to think of the cost; we would have to meet it from somewhere. We had no choice. As night fell, the front of the villa was bathed in the light of a vast bonfire as the sound of drumming, piping, singing, dancing and laughter rose to the heavens. It was a strangely wonderful sight.

There was just one problem. Andreas was absent and as the evening wore on, I became more and more worried. Despina was, too. She'd been scanning the party, in vain, for the eldest son. 'Where is he?' she asked me, anxiously.

'He was up in the mountains checking out the woods for deer hunting. Or so they say. But he should have been back by now. Long before, in fact. The whole region must know we are celebrating something.'

'So why isn't he here?'

'You know why. Because he wants to make a point.'

Sparks flew up from the bonfire and I could see my Lord Theodore, his arm round his second son, strolling, greeting people and being greeted.

'By the way, I'm sorry if I was rude this morning,' she said, under her breath. 'I do admire the way you run things.'

On this strangest of days, I was beginning to see many things in a different light, Despina included. 'No, I am sorry,' I replied. 'I gave you the wrong answer. I've been a steward for too long. It has corrupted the way I see the world. I judge everything in terms of its effect on the estate, not in human terms at all.'

'That is dangerous,' she replied.

I was about to agree – I couldn't have agreed more, in fact – when one of Hendrik's men came over and tugged at my elbow. 'Master Andreas is waiting outside,' he said in a coarse whisper that smelled of roasted chicken.

'Thank you,' I replied. 'Excuse me, Despina.' And as I jostled through the crowd, I realised I had addressed 'Miss Despina' the colleague as a friend for the first time. It felt strangely good, like the party itself.

Andreas, however, could have no truck with the air of forgiveness. Standing alone outside, his fury and contempt for the proceedings were written across his face for all to see. I bowed. 'Master Andreas, we have been awaiting you. Please, your presence is an honour,' I said as I motioned to the door more in hope than realistic expectation.

'I'll be damned if I'll come in,' he stormed. 'My brother is back and my father treats him as if he was a prince.'

'Sir,' I said, pushing my luck, 'it would be good if you would come in.' Something about today was helping me to live dangerously for a change.

'Out of my way, Francis!' he raged, and bundled me aside. There he stood in the open doorway, burning with anger and jealousy, facing the party head on. Who knows if he'd been planning this scene? I have to admit, though, that it was an impressive stand all the same. He was a great oak of a man and the doorway framed him like a picture of strength. I stood behind him, my bravado draining away like a spilled glass of wine. The morning's events were bad enough, but this threatened to be worse.

'*Stop this nonsense!*' Andreas shouted, cutting straight through the din of the festivities. Within a second, every drum, pipe and voice had fallen silent.

He bellowed again. 'My brother is a fool who has brought shame on us all. He should be punished. He wasted my money, our money, *your* money, on *whores*.' The crowd took a sharp intake of breath. 'He took our honour and trampled it in the dirt. Now my father wishes to restore him.' He hurled the words angrily into the room.

And there, from out of nowhere, was Theodore – standing before his son, the same loving look in his eye that had extended to Yiannis. 'Andreas, my dear son,' he said gently. 'You must understand. Your brother was lost. I had given him up for dead. He is now alive. Celebration is the only thing that is right.'

For one terrible moment, I thought Andreas would strike his father and I moved closer to intervene, but he lowered his face until it was just inches away from his father's and snarled at him. 'Right? *Right?! This* is not *right!* You've never treated me like this. Yet this drifter son of yours gets a *party*.'

'My dear son, *he* was lost.'

'I have worked for you and for this estate every day for years. I have always obeyed your orders and you have never, ever given me this attention.' A sole tear threatened to betray just how much this was hurting him, as he choked out his words.

'My son,' Theodore spoke with such kindness. 'You must give up this lie that I love you less. I love you. I would search for you as I searched for your brother. Everything I have is yours. Do not be deaf to my voice calling you now, to join us and eat.'

But Andreas would have none of it. He turned on his heels and slammed the great door shut. Theodore stood rooted, calm, as all eyes turned towards him. I nodded to the minstrels. Music flowed into the vacuum left by Andreas and slowly, and unsteadily, the celebrations began again.

I placed guards around the villa that night in case Andreas tried something foolish, but in the morning word reached me that he had left for the city.

I arranged to meet Despina in the grounds of the villa under the apple trees, which were now thick with blossom. Amid the turmoil, she and she alone seemed to make sense of things. She saw the world from a different angle. And she helped me to open my eyes.

'How terrible,' I said to her. 'He gets one son back and loses the other.'

She gave me that strange, knowing look and shook her head. 'No. He had lost both of them. Now he has found one and the other realises that he is lost.'

I thought about it and realised she was right. 'Despina, will he get Andreas back?'

She smiled, sadly, looking down. 'I am flattered and honoured that you think I can answer such a question. But, of course, I cannot.'

Over the next few days and weeks we slowly settled down. Gossip was rife, of course, about Yiannis's return and Andreas's departure, and the Prince sent an emissary to find out what had happened for himself. I didn't see him because Theodore spoke with him alone, telling him that it was family business and that – with all respect – it did not really have any relevance to the Prince. Then he sent him back on his way.

Yiannis began to recover from the rigours of his year away. He put on some weight and started to look like his old self again; yet his manner was much changed. He was now a quieter and more reflective man. One day I was walking through the villa gardens after meeting with Theodore, and I came across him sitting on a seat. He gestured to me urgently to come and sit next to him. I joined him, feeling awkward because I was sure that he knew how I felt about things.

He turned to me. 'Francis, I want to thank you.'

I was genuinely taken aback. 'Whatever for?'

'You handled my return very well. I realise, now, that it could have gone disastrously.'

'Yes, it nearly did,' I said, thoughtfully. 'Crowds are a funny thing. But you need to thank your father.'

'I have. But you helped a lot. You have both showed me such grace. I am so unworthy and yet you and my father have treated me with such respect.'

'Thank you.' I felt ashamed as I knew that I hadn't respected him. 'But my job is to do the best that I can for the estate and for your father.'

He raised an eyebrow. 'I know your feelings. But that doesn't matter to me. You were right and I was wrong. I was a fool.' A servant is not used to receiving apologies from their master, and I didn't know what to say. So I mumbled something along the lines that I quite understood, and I was sorry if my attitude had been wrong, and I was glad that he had been reconciled with his father.

'What are your plans now?' I asked.

'I was expecting to join the servants, to pay off something of my debts. But my father refuses to allow it.'

'He is a truly remarkable man,' I noted.

'Indeed. I'm thinking of leaving,' he said. 'But with my father's blessing this time. I think I can earn a living in the city teaching. All those books I used to read! Maybe Andreas will come back if I'm out of the way. My father would like that.'

I looked at him. He was clearly a changed man. 'Master Yiannis, you may like to know that I, er, I made an error in giving you your money last year. After you had gone, I found that there was a sizeable amount left. It is in an account for you . . . should you require it.'

He smiled with grateful eyes. 'What a very convenient over-sight. Thank you. It may well come in useful.'

A week later, helped by the money I had saved for him, Yiannis moved to the city, where he started teaching. Over the next few months, I was pleased to hear that it was going well. Of course, there was never any question of him paying off his debts – he would have to teach for a hundred years to do that – but it was a start. I was pleased to hear that he kept in touch with his father through regular correspondence.

A few days after Yiannis departed, Andreas returned and set himself up in the far end of the villa, as far away as possible from his father. I do not know whether they even spoke to each other. I certainly never saw them together after that dreadful encounter at the party. From the little revealed by Despina, she found herself employed very much as an intermediary.

As summer drifted once more into autumn, and autumn chilled to winter, this uneasy situation continued. Then, in the first weeks of the new year, it became apparent that Theodore was not well. The strains of the previous months had surely taken their toll, as had the constant, malevolent presence of Andreas around the estate.

In the second month of the year, Theodore descended into violent fits of coughing. We summoned a specialist doctor from the city and Yiannis made his way rapidly back to seek his father, being careful to keep out of the way of his brother. As I paid the doctor the usual extortionate rate for such a professional, I asked him privately for his verdict. He looked around to make sure no one else was listening, and shook his head. 'He is coughing blood,' he whispered. 'You should make sure that his affairs are in order. His care now belongs more with the priests than with doctors.'

A few days hence, I was summoned to Theodore's room. There I found a thin, pale-faced man who seemed to have aged ten years in the last month. His doctor sat at the back of the room, keeping watch.

Theodore motioned me over to his bedside. His face may have changed, but those penetrating eyes had not lost their look of love. 'Francis,' he said in a low, slurred voice. 'I want to thank you for your faithfulness to me. I have not been the easiest of masters to serve. I know you have, on occasions, disagreed with me – but you've always been faithful to my house, and I wish you well.'

I bowed my head; to receive such praise from your master is the greatest thing that any steward can hope for. I had done my job.

'Do you know, Francis, why I acted as I did?'

'No, Sir.'

He put a blood-stained cloth to his lips and coughed violently. 'I could only try to act in the way that God acts.' He caught my look of puzzlement.

'You don't understand, do you? Despina does. You must talk to her.'

He coughed again, painfully, and took a sip of water from a glass.

'God gives us freedom even though it breaks his heart, Francis.' Theodore was not a religious man, yet to hear him talk of God like this began to make sense.

I nodded, slowly.

'You think I made myself look like a fool by taking back my son in such a way, don't you?' We had not spoken of those events until now.

'That is not a word I would ever use of you, Sir. Now, or ever.'

Theodore managed a smile. 'Diplomatic to the end, Francis. But I was a fool. I lost honour, I lowered myself – *running* – good grief.' He shook his head slowly. 'I can barely believe it myself. But it was my way of saving Yiannis.'

I nodded again.

'You see, I love him, as I do both of my sons; I love them so much. No price was too high to bring Yiannis back, not even our reputation.' There was that word again. Reputation. He looked at me, smiling. 'When you have a child, Francis, you will understand. Whatever those men do cannot change the fact that they are my sons, and my love for them does not depend on their actions. It will not change.'

I was silent. My Lord continued.

'And you saw the mob, Francis. What would have happened if I had delayed? If I had walked steadily, as is deemed fit and proper?'

'I think, Sir, they would have driven him out. Thrown stones. They were angry at what had happened – at the way he'd acted. And some of them had lost their land.'

'Yes, the mob would have given him justice all right. As they saw fit.' He closed his eyes in pain. 'God preserve us from such justice, Francis. The justice we deserve. Where would any of us be if God used justice alone as a measure?'

I paused. My life seemed to flash before me and I felt the truth of what he said. 'Indeed, Sir,' was all I could muster.

'I saved him, Francis. At a cost.'

'Yes, you saved your son, Sir. He's a different man now.'

'I'm glad. Do not the priests teach – although I fear they have forgotten it themselves – that God became a man and was mocked? And worse, he was stripped and nailed to a cross, so that he might save his sons from their own mess?'

'They do, Sir. But I have never understood it.'

He looked gently at me. 'My prayer is that you will. God chose to be humbled because he loves you. Me? I was merely mocked as a fool. And perhaps that is all I am.'

He seemed to struggle, but turned to look at me again.

'You have to take the first step back, Francis. You have to decide to return.' His eyes bore a great sadness, but also hope; his voice, now, was almost a whisper. 'The distance is the same for us all, whether it's from a wild rebellion obvious for all to see or just a cold, sim-mering resentment and self-pity, trapped in the quietness of a heart.'

He coughed again and the doctor came forward from the other end of the room to order me out. Theodore closed his eyes and motioned me back. 'But if you return, he will meet you along the way.' A faint smile broke. He was already leaving for another place – in his heart he was probably running again, this time along the road that his beloved Katerina had taken so many years before. I closed my eyes and, for a moment, I could see another figure in the distance, charging out to welcome him home. I squeezed his hand and, with a heavy heart, kissed him goodbye.

He died two days later and when I heard the news, I wept as if I had lost my own father. We buried him, according to our custom, within forty-eight hours. The religious rituals seemed peculiarly unhelpful; the priests, as ever, spoke a lot about duty and honour and very little about grace and forgiveness. There was a curious, perfunctory nature about the way they conducted the service, as if they were anxious to end the era of embarrassment. I closed my eyes and thought of my dead master. I treasured the picture of him being welcomed home by his Father. 'He will meet you along the way . . .' Theodore's words will never leave me.

At the graveside, where the ground was as hard as ice and the sky a perfect, crystal blue, representatives had gathered from the neighbouring families. As I watched them, it was clear that their fine words and solemn expressions betrayed no great sadness. Andreas took a prominent role in events and was dressed in the finest clothes and wore gold rings on his fingers. He looked around with eyes that spoke of mastery and control, not grief. Something about his pose and manner seemed deliberately designed to reassure everyone present that, with him, things were back as they ought to be. Theodore had gone; everyone's world could return to normal. In contrast, Yiannis was standing at the edge of the day, craving insignificance and bearing a painful, honest grief.

And the common people? Well, they gathered around, keeping their respectful distance as was right and proper. Were they, I wondered, genuinely sad? I couldn't tell; I don't think they had ever really understood Theodore. Some of the wiser ones were, I thought, troubled, not so much by the loss of Theodore but by what – or who – was to come after him. Indeed, as I glanced at Andreas, tall, proud and taking stock with cold eyes, I felt a shiver of fear.

As soon as the first clods of earth were shovelled onto the grave, I was not surprised to see Yiannis slipping away rapidly. He gave me a smile, raised a hand in a half-salute of respect, and left.

Two days later I was summoned into the presence of Andreas. Things had already changed at the house. There was now a guard at the door who demanded to know my business and whether I had an appointment. I ignored the insult, but when I had got past him I found myself before a clerk who consulted a list. Only then was I ushered into the presence of Lord Andreas. He had taken little time in establishing an office in his father's old study. The books, the worn carpet and the comfortable chairs had gone, and the old battered desk had been replaced by a shiny new one that seemed bigger and taller. Andreas sat behind it in a high-backed chair that might as well have been a throne.

I sat before him on a new, hard seat and he stared at me with calculating brown eyes. 'You served my father,' he said, and there was an unspoken question in his words.

'And, if it is your will, I will serve you,' I replied. 'I joined the Salvadori estate before you were born and the interests of your house have been mine ever since.'

He looked straight into my eyes; I think he was trying to intimidate me. 'Francis, know this. I am not my father. My father governed in a way that was lax. There will be changes.'

I gave a little bow of my head to acknowledge the truth of this, but said nothing; I had decided to watch my words. Once upon a time, this might have been music to my ears. Now I was not so sure.

He leaned back in his chair, watching me as a cat might watch a mouse. 'Three changes to start with. First, I want you to go over the accounts of the last twenty years and find every case in which my father was lenient. I want you to present me with those records a week from today. I am going to call in those debts.'

I nodded, fighting back the temptation to show my anger. 'It can be done,' I said slowly, battling the emotion in my voice.

'Second, I want all the tenancy agreements reviewed. My desire is to buy back the land that fool of a brother of mine lost. And to do that, I need to have the money. Put a 10 per cent surcharge on them all.'

He did not ask me what I thought. In fact, I knew he did not care what I thought. This was just as well, as I did not trust myself to answer him.

'And third, there is the issue of the common land. As you know, it has been a tradition that the people of the town may use it to graze their animals. But there is too much common land; some of it is too good to waste. Again, in a week's time, let me have a map of the common land and let us see what they don't need.'

Again, I simply nodded. 'Is there anything else, Sir?'

'No, not for the moment. A week today. Remember.'

I got to my feet. 'You may be assured, my Lord, that, as ever, my interest is the honour of your family.' He didn't shake hands, but sent me away with a dismissive gesture.

Instead of returning to the office, I went back to my house and lay on the bed thinking. I had never been a praying man, though I had always mouthed the routine prayers imposed by the priests. But there on the bed I prayed for the first time. I asked for wisdom, courage and guidance. And whether my prayers were answered or not, I began to sense that I knew what I must do. Don't ask me how.

I arose, and headed back to the office as if it was business as usual. Once there, I scribbled a single-lined note, sealed it and summoned a boy to deliver it. Then, with a heavy heart, I ordered that the first files of the last twenty years be delivered to my desk. That evening, after supper, I returned to my office and began to work through the oldest of them.

It was a bitter night, sprinkled with flurries of snow, and I knew there would be few people around. Just after eight, by my reckoning, the door creaked open and Despina's snow-kissed face appeared around it. She smiled. I locked the door behind her, pulled up two chairs by the fire and threw on another log.

We sat facing each other, and she slowly took her scarf and gloves off as a few last snowflakes melted into her hair.

'Thank you for coming, Despina,' I said.

'I presume you have your reasons.'

I nodded. 'Things are changing.'

'And not for the better.' Her face looked sad for a moment, but the melancholy gave way to a mischievous smile. 'But Francis, you can adapt, can't you? Doesn't the good steward adjust to the change of a master?'

I returned the smile.

'I talked with Andreas this morning. I –'

She raised a finger in interruption. 'Don't you mean "my Lord Andreas"?'

'No, I do not. I was looking for a sign, Despina. Andreas obliged thrice over. He gave me three demands, all of which would have horrified his father. All of which horrify me.' I paused. 'And so, having spent over half my life here, it is time for me to leave.' I had no idea how Despina would react, but I braced myself.

'Where will you go?' she asked with an urgency that encouraged me.

'I have made no decision yet. The city, to begin with. Our late, beloved Lord Theodore gave me a wooden box in his will, full of gold crowns. There was also a small piece of paper on which he had written, "You may need this."'

She nodded and I guessed that he had been similarly generous to her.

'I have to say, Despina, that I am adjusting my views of the Lord Theodore. I took him for granted while he lived, but now he is gone and I have seen who has taken his place, I miss him more than I ever thought I would.'

Tears began to form in her eyes.

'I was thinking,' I said, 'about possibly buying a farm, a smallholding. Nothing much. I have been careful here and have saved some money. With that and my Lord's gift, I can manage. I would need labour, but I think it will work. So I will write my letter of resignation tomorrow and leave.'

'When?'

'Tomorrow evening. I will leave my resignation on my desk and slip away unnoticed.'

'I see.'

'I wanted to ask, do you have any plans?'

She stared at the fire. 'No, I do not think I will stay here long. Like you, I have already seen the signs. He struck one of the girls yesterday. Andreas seems to care little for all that his father held dear. In fact, he seems to delight in trampling on it.'

There was one last part to my plan, and I suddenly became aware of my heart beating madly. Blood was rushing through my ears. Was I mad? I had truly changed. 'I was wondering if you would come with me?'

Mischief and longing crossed her features. 'Francis.' She paused. 'Is that a business proposition or something more personal?'

'Actually . . .' I took a deep breath. 'It was meant as a proposal of marriage.'

'Are you so desperate that you are proposing to contaminate the fine family name of Nutrizio with my own?' She knew how to make me squirm.

'I have decided, rather belatedly, that there is more to life than honour,' I muttered. 'Despina . . . will you marry me?'

She paused for a moment – which felt like a lifetime. 'Francis, if you'd asked me previously, I would have taken no time in politely declining your offer. I have found you heartless and cold.'

I bowed my head, trying to hide my embarrassment. 'A fair assessment of me indeed. May I ask you for forgiveness?'

'Granted, of course. But I'm fussy. I want a husband and a lover, not a steward.' I felt nervous and uneasy. My usual composure abandoned me and I was humbled. 'But,' she added, 'I think you've changed.'

'Oh, I hope so!' I cried, honestly. 'I've done so much thinking recently about the brothers and their situation. I was critical – very critical – of Yiannis, and what he did was not right. Still, I have come to a conclusion. Every one of us is like him or Andreas. We are all, in our different ways, lost. But God has bought our forgiveness and restoration at an enormous cost. His unreserved and unlimited love is offered wholly and equally to both sons. We either accept that – as Yiannis did – or we reject it.'

'Ah, the penny has dropped!' There was wonderment and joy on her face.

'I'm a slow learner. But from what I can see, Andreas has rejected it. He might have stayed at home, but he was lost all along. He refused to come home from a cold anger and self-pity that has made him such a stranger to his family. It seems that to reject this forgiveness is to choose a hard path.' I paused. 'How slow I am. I didn't –'

'Yes.'

'Yes?'

'Yes, I *will* marry you. You have changed.'

I didn't realise how much I needed to hear Despina say those words until she did. It was a sort of homecoming in itself. Of course, looking back on this breathless night, I know now that I had grown to love her. But love, like life, is a strange creature. It's only when you look back along the road, sometimes, that you find you've taken that turn.

Despina gazed into the fire. Little needed to be said.

'But which way do we go?'

For once, neither of us had an answer.

And so I returned to this very room, the backdrop to so many years, knowing that everything that had gone before had brought me to this point of no return. I was leaving – we were leaving – and the road that stretched out ahead was unfamiliar, less travelled.

My letter of resignation did not take long to write. I packed those few things that I wanted to take with me. And then I began on this story: an exorcism, a baptism, a moment of sudden clarity that has taken so long, yet come so quickly.

Five short, blunt words. Beating at the door, ringing in my ears, shouting at the window on a dark, clear night; driving me to God-knows-where, to a place I might have glimpsed, but not yet seen; bereft of grid reference or signpost.

Which way do we go?

Wherever it takes us, this road less travelled, this sacred path, one thing I now believe with all my heart: we're going home, however long it might take, whoever we might encounter. And me? I'm running as fast as my legs will carry me. It is time.

PART TWO

PART TWO

Introduction

The story of the Salvadori family that you have just read is based on a story Jesus told, which is recorded in Luke's Gospel (Luke 15:11–32). This story or parable is traditionally titled 'The Prodigal Son', although, as you may soon notice, it is as much about the father and the elder brother. (To be a 'prodigal', incidentally, means to spend money recklessly and wastefully.) Although many modern Bible versions talk about it as the 'Parable of the Lost Son', we will use the traditional title here.

In a modern translation the account of the Prodigal reads as follows:

Jesus continued: 'There was a man who had two sons. The younger one said to his father, "Father, give me my share of the estate." So he divided his property between them.

'Not long after that, the younger son got together all he had, set off for a distant country and there squandered his wealth in wild living. After he had spent everything, there was a severe famine in that whole country, and he began to be in need. So he went and hired himself out to a citizen of that country, who sent him to his fields to feed pigs. He longed to fill his stomach with the pods that the pigs were eating, but no one gave him anything.

'When he came to his senses, he said, "How many of my father's hired servants have food to spare, and here I am starving to death! I will set out and go back to my father and say to him: Father, I have sinned against heaven and against you. I am no longer worthy to be called your son; make me like one of your hired servants." So he got up and went to his father.

'But while he was still a long way off, his father saw him and was filled with compassion for him; he ran to his son, threw his arms around him and kissed him.

'The son said to him, "Father, I have sinned against heaven and against you. I am no longer worthy to be called your son."

'But the father said to his servants, "Quick! Bring the best robe and put it on him. Put a ring on his finger and sandals on his feet. Bring the fattened calf and kill it. Let's have a feast and celebrate. For this son of mine was dead and is alive again; he was lost and is found." So they began to celebrate.

'Meanwhile, the older son was in the field. When he came near the house, he heard music and dancing. So he called one of the servants and asked him what was going on. "Your brother has come," he replied, "and your father has killed the fattened calf because he has him back safe and sound."

'The older brother became angry and refused to go in. So his father went out and pleaded with him. But he answered his father, "Look! All these years I've been slaving for you and never disobeyed your orders. Yet you never gave me even a young goat so I could celebrate with my friends. But when this son of yours who has squandered your property with prostitutes comes home, you kill the fattened calf for him!"'

(Luke 15:11–30)

By any reckoning, this is an extraordinary story. The Prodigal Son has inspired poems, operas, plays and books and a number of art works (including no fewer than four by Rembrandt). The Prodigal Son is not just one of the longest and most detailed of all Jesus' parables, but for many people is the greatest of them; it is certainly the most commented on and, perhaps, the best known.

The story of the Prodigal is loved for its universality. Human beings have not changed and the three characters are instantly recognisable: most of us have known the prodigal, the father and the elder brother; some of us have been them, and some of us are them now. Although today's prodigal might have left a farewell message on Facebook, sold his share of the estate on eBay and flown to the far country, he is clearly recognisable in this ancient document.

The story of the Prodigal and his family is loved for its intelligibility. Some of the other parables have enigmatic cultural and religious details that render them obscure to us. Here, at least on the surface, we have the very simplest of stories: we all know what is going on. Or at least we think we do.

The story of the Prodigal is also loved for its literary quality. Charles Dickens reputedly called it the greatest short story ever written in English.[1] The story presses many emotional buttons, yet somehow retains its artistic integrity. The tone is involving and touching without ever being sentimental. It is of a perfect length: short enough to be instantly understood, but long enough to involve us. There is not a word wasted, yet there are tiny details (the hunger that makes pig food seem attractive, the father who runs, the elder son's brusque summons of the servant) that bring life to the narrative.

Perhaps the supreme achievement of the Parable of the Prodigal is its psychological authenticity. There must be very few of us who did not at some stage of our youth feel like walking out on our parents. There can be very few parents who have not known the agony of yielding to the wishes of a child knowing that acquiescence will almost certainly lead to disaster. There must be many of us who can identify closely with the hurt pride of the elder brother. This authenticity drags us in, allowing us to identify with the characters. We find ourselves living in the story and filling in the blanks with our own imagination.

It is this very virtue of involvement that raises problems. Writers and speakers who are normally very careful seem to throw caution to the winds when they come to this parable and seem unable to avoid adding to it – expanding on the probable relationship between the brothers, fleshing out the social setting of the family and explaining the psychology of why things have gone so badly wrong between younger son and father. Now there is nothing wrong with this; indeed, as we shall see, one of the characteristics of parables is to invite exactly such involvement. Yet if we are not careful we dangerously blur the boundary between interpretation and imagination. One reason why this book is written the way it is, is to allow us to separate these two elements. So, whereas in Part One you were presented with a freely imagined fleshing out of the parable, this second part is a much more restrained examination of what the parable says and means. Indeed, let's make a distinction between the biblical Parable of the Prodigal Son and the story of the crisis in the House of Salvadori with which we began the book. The first is God's word; the second is ours. Only the original is authoritative. Of course, we have done our best to stay faithful to the themes of Jesus' original, but an inevitable result of expanding Jesus' original story (which, in most English translations, is no more than 450 words long) is that we have made additions and modifications. The very fact that we have updated it by a dozen or more centuries and moved it around the shores of the Mediterranean into southern Europe should alert readers to the fact that they are reading something that is not what was once called 'Holy Writ'.

In this section, then, we want to leave the imaginary world of the Salvadoris and turn to Jesus' original story and look at it carefully. That word *carefully* has two meanings and we use them both: we want to look at it in detail and we want to handle it with care. As we have already noted, the very popularity of this parable has caused problems. Some writers and speakers have so teased, tugged and added to the story that its original shape has become distorted beyond recognition. Yet there are places where we can confidently go beyond the text, because this is not a story in isolation. It links in with a vast weight of other teaching, both from Jesus and from elsewhere in the New Testament. Indeed, as we will see, it is a story that neatly ties together the world of Jesus with that of the preaching of the early church.

We will say here very little about the author of this parable. We have already written a book together on Jesus and his teaching (*The Life: A Portrait of Jesus*) and, rather than expand this treatment of the parable to try to cover everything, we are happy to refer you to that. Nevertheless, you will find that he looms large over this section. You would hardly expect otherwise.

In the following chapters we want to look at various aspects of the Parable of the Prodigal. In chapter 1 we examine the background to the story, in chapter 2 we look at the fascinating issue of whether or not the parable really does go back to Jesus of Nazareth, while in chapter 3 we turn our attention to parables and why Jesus used them. Then in chapter 4 we discuss the setting of the Parable of the Prodigal, and in chapters 5, 6 and 7 we look at what we will call the three acts of the parable, dominated respectively by the younger son, the father and the elder son. Finally, we will bring together some conclusions. Apart from some asides, we will reserve practical applications for the third section of this book.

You will find that the discussions in these pages range more widely than just this parable. One attractive feature of the Parable of the Prodigal that we have barely hinted at so far is that it deals with much that is at the very heart of the gospel. The result is that in thinking about this parable we find ourselves not on the periphery of the good news, but close to its centre. There are many matters this story raises and some of them are amongst the most important things we can ever think about.

1

The Background to the Prodigal

THE WORLD OF THE PRODIGAL

To fully understand this parable you need to do your best to get yourself into the mindset and culture of the time. Our world is so dominated by technology that it is easy to assume that the only real difference between us and Jesus' contemporaries in Palestine* is technological. True, the fact that we have phones, email and televisions and they didn't is a factor. After all, when the Prodigal went into that 'distant country' he was effectively cut off from all contact. Yet there are more subtle things than technology that separate us from the world of this parable. One reason for writing the story of the House of Salvadori was to explore some of these aspects. We'd like to suggest that there are three things you need to bear in mind about the world of the Prodigal.

The first thing is that it was a world in which God and morality mattered. It is easy to overlook this, because when we look at any historical figures, not just those in the Bible, we tend to assume that their past was the same as our present. (Hollywood is, of course, often grotesquely guilty of this, but the error is more widespread.) The gulf between our Western culture and that of the

---

* It's worth making the point that, in common with most writers on biblical matters, we use the term *Palestine* for the land and *Israel* for the Jewish nation.

parable is particularly major in the area of religious beliefs and the importance people attributed to them. In Jesus' culture (as with most societies outside the West today) atheism was rare. Almost everybody believed in a god or (especially if you were influenced by the Greeks and Romans) gods, who ran the world and who would sort things out at some last terrible day of judgement. 'Where will you spend eternity?' was not a bizarre bumper sticker question, but a challenge that overshadowed the existence of most men and women.

The inevitable implication of a belief in a great day of reckoning was that doing right in the eyes of God was essential. Religion was not a peripheral matter reserved for an hour or so on a day when you didn't feel like staying in bed and reading the Sunday papers; it was the hub around which your very existence rotated. In the world of the Gospels, most men and women took matters of faith just as seriously. So when we read of the issues between Jesus and the Pharisees, let's be clear that we are not referring to minor details of social etiquette, but to something that was, in truth, far more important than life and death.

The second thing we need to grasp is that, even pushing the religious element of life to one side, the first hearers of the story of the Prodigal had very different priorities from us. For one thing, like much of the developing world today, theirs was a rural environment. The setting of all Jesus' parables is that of the country-side of Palestine, and specifically the northern area, Galilee. In the parables we glimpse farmers scattering seed on thin soils, women searching for coins in dark, windowless stone houses and fishermen bending over nets at the lakeside. Such a setting is not only distant from us, it is also distant from Paul, who, in the letters of the New Testament, draws his imagery from the urban Greek world of temple, theatre and the sports arena. The rural Galilee of the parables is a geographically limited world. The devout and their families might, on special occasions, make the long pilgrimage up to Jerusalem far to the south, but otherwise men and women lived out their days without travelling beyond the horizon. Theirs was a world of subsistence agriculture, with a few large landowners and many peasants who, Sabbaths excepted, worked from dawn to dusk. Life here teetered precariously on the very edge of existence; the slightest change in the pattern of unpredictable winds or rain brought drought, disease and death. One other difference existed (and it underlies this parable): for Jewish farmers of the time the country-side was not just land, but *their* land. The Jewish faith held that, in a real sense, you didn't own the land, but instead you merely leased it from God.[1] To sell such a heritage was an act that betrayed past generations and endangered future ones.

The very precarious nature of this world (heightened, of course, by the absence of any social security or health care) meant that everybody depended on the family. That is why there are so many biblical injunctions to care for the widows and orphans: in this world to be without a family is to be, in every sense, bankrupt. And here of course family was not just mum, dad and a couple of kids. It was the extended family with its interlocking tangle of grandparents, uncles, aunts and innumerable cousins. Such families actually have something of the business about them: in this sort of fragile existence you never know when you're going to need an uncle for a loan, a cousin for help with the crops or an aunt to cook for a celebration. The edifice of Jewish society was constructed with the bricks, not of individuals, but of families. These families were linked into clans, the clans into tribes and the tribes into the torn, battered and turbulent structure of the Jewish nation. Then, as now, in such societies the family links needed to be vigorously enforced. A family either sticks together or it falls together: in the merciless battle of life, to fail your family is to betray them. So everybody is aware of these links and society builds in ways to reward those who keep them and punish those who break them. One of the more difficult pieces of Old Testament legislation which we need to keep in mind when we look at the Parable of the Prodigal is Deuteronomy 21:18–21, which commands the stoning of rebellious sons. Even if it was something of a piece of hypothetical legislation (there is no record of this penalty ever being carried out), it says a lot about how such a culture viewed family solidarity. In the tight-knit fabric of such a family-based society, a son's rebellion might be that single tiny rip that spreads unstoppably into the slash that tears everything apart. It was akin to a soldier's desertion on the field of battle and had to be tackled with a similar severity.

The third difference from us – well, most of us – is that there was another bonding agent to this society, and this is something that we need to understand because it underlies much of the story of the Prodigal. It is an all-pervading social code based on honour and shame. We who live in the modern, urbanised, anonymous West all too frequently misunderstand what is happening in cultures where shame and honour are key factors. This is unfortunate, as our failure to understand such cultures (and they are present today over much of the world outside Western Europe, North America and Australasia) can often have very real and disastrous consequences. In a shame and honour culture, life centres on the twin demands of avoiding shame and gaining honour. Honour is linked with accumulating social status and praise from within the culture; shame is linked with losing it. To be known as a personal friend of the mayor, to have a son who is a surgeon, to have a house that is visibly larger than everybody else's: these are all things that bring one honour. To be missed off the wedding-of-the-year invitation list, to have a son who fails college, or to have a daughter – heaven forbid – who gets pregnant outside marriage: these are all things which incur shame.*

* In such cultures, a woman's honour and shame are almost exclusively associated with keeping sexual standards and producing children (preferably boys).

The result is that life is essentially a never-ending game of snakes and ladders, in which you must scramble up the short ladders of honour while dodging around the long snakes of shame. Everything is about honour and saving face. Think of an everyday situation such as going into a work meeting full of people and seeing an empty chair next to a couple of your bosses. Do you try to take the seat? In the West we might well make our decision simply based on whether we like their company or whether we prefer to sit with friends. In a shame and honour culture the criteria would be very different. If your bosses accept you, then you have gained honour; if they reject you ('Oh, *sorry*, we're keeping the seat for someone else'), then you have suffered public shame. It doesn't make life easy.

The matter of honour and shame affects everything, including speech. After all, words can confer both honour and shame. (That is why trying to do a deal or pursue negotiations in places like the Middle East can take what seems like forever: woe betide the man or woman who tries to force someone into losing face!) As we will see, one reason why parables are often used is that they allow a message to be given without a direct and honour-threatening confrontation.

Avoiding shame can often overrule any issue of right or wrong. Indeed, as we are becoming all too unhappily aware, in such cultures the need to avoid family shame can sometimes be powerful enough to make it necessary for a son or daughter who has committed some 'wrong' to be put to death in an 'honour killing' so that the act of shame may be erased. The honour of the family must be upheld. A grotesque story Chris heard from the Lebanese Civil War makes the point. A Western journalist was on the front line between two warring communities, interviewing a sniper. Eventually it emerged that the man was being paid on the basis of how many members of the opposite sect he killed. 'I see,' said the journalist, trying to hide his feelings of revulsion. 'And when you tell your boss the figure, how does he know that you are telling him the truth?' The sniper looked up from his gun, his face filled with indignant fury. 'How dare you suggest such a thing! I am an honourable man.'

These issues of honour and shame – unnoticed by many Westerners – run throughout the Bible and underlie many of the parables. As we will find out, they are critical to understanding this parable in particular.

It is easy to criticise this sort of culture. It can have a horrendous effect on individuals, not least on women. It is also a culture where nothing that depends on honest and open evaluation of the truth can thrive: so such matters as science, education and the media creak and groan under the impossible task of having to seek honour and avoid shame. Yet the hard rule of honour has its strengths: it creates societies that are extraordinarily stable and well ordered. Their town centres do not become no-go areas after nightfall!

Some academic theologians, secure in urban universities in Western Europe and America, have expressed scepticism that the present shame and honour culture in the Middle East can be safely extrapolated back two thousand years, given that the area has become largely Islamic in this time. Two comments are worth making. The first is that these sorts of cultural values are assumed throughout the New Testament. In the Gospels it can be seen right from the angelic announcement to Mary (Luke 1:26–38; Matthew 1:18–25), where matters of her shame and Joseph's honour are central, to the cross, which is explicitly referred to by Paul in terms of shame (Philippians 2:5–8). In fact, the reason why the Romans crucified people was not so much because it was very painful and fatal (which would be an adequate deterrent for most of us), but because the often naked victim suffered prolonged public humiliation and so brought shame on the family. In this case, crucifixion was truly a fate worse than death. A second point is that the shame and honour culture is widespread around the Mediterranean (as J.John has experienced personally in regard to his marriage and his work), even in areas untouched by Islam. The history of the Middle East is studded with the sad accounts of soldiers, politicians, industrialists and ordinary people who made the fatal mistake – sometimes quite literally so – of taking a statement to be true when it was merely a measure to avoid shame.*

With these points in mind, let us now turn to the parable itself.

---

* When Chris was doing geological fieldwork in Lebanon, he came within ten yards of being blown up by an Israeli helicopter gunship on the slopes of Mount Hermon and was then arrested by the United Nations, because his local guide couldn't bring himself to admit that he really didn't know where the Lebanese border ended and the free-fire zone began. He apparently took the view that the risk of death was preferable to a shameful admission of ignorance. Chris did not share this opinion.

2

The Origins of the Parable of the Prodigal

For some of you reading this book, it may be enough for you to know that the story of the Prodigal is a parable of Jesus recorded in the Bible. For you, that is the end of the matter. But there may be others who feel compelled to say, 'How do we know that this really did come from the mouth of Jesus?' They may even want to explore the possibility that it is some sort of traditional tale passed down over centuries, only to be borrowed and rebranded by creative early Christians as a story told by their Messiah. So here we want to justify our belief that this story does indeed go back to Jesus. If this is not an issue with you, feel free to skip this chapter.

The main justification for spending time arguing for the parable's authenticity is simply that it teaches so much that is extraordinarily revealing about the nature of God. If we are going to base our lives on the truth it illuminates, then we need to be certain of its legitimacy. Sadly, we live in a sceptical age when it is simply not good enough to say 'It is in the Bible', as if that ended the discussion.

So, even allowing for the translation of Jesus' original story from the Aramaic in which he taught* to the Greek in which the New

---

* Three languages operated in the Palestine of Jesus' day: Hebrew, Aramaic and Greek. Which of the first two languages he used to teach in is debated; it was probably Aramaic.

Testament is written, do we have his very words? After all, it is not uncommon to hear people today confidently offer the opinion that much of what we know about Jesus is a creation of the early church. So, for instance, books such as Dan Brown's *The Da Vinci Code* claim that much of Jesus' teaching – and many of the facts about him – was created by these early Christians. Somehow, it is alleged, early followers of Jesus put together fragments of teaching from this Jewish teacher and elaborated them until they had produced the Gospels we have today.* With that in mind, let's look at what we know about the parable.

LUKE AND HIS GOSPEL

The Parable of the Prodigal is only found in Luke's Gospel. That isn't too surprising. Luke – who had something of a flair for narrative himself – has a soft spot for parables; around two-thirds of all Jesus' parables occur in his Gospel. The account of the Prodigal occurs as the deliberate finale of three related parables in chapter 15. (By the way, the business of dividing up the text with numbered chapters and verses took place over a thousand years later.†) The New Testament starts with four Gospels, all giving accounts of the life, death and resurrection of Jesus the Messiah ('Jesus the

---

* It's impossible to avoid commenting on the fact that when people read something they like in the Gospels (such as 'the promise of heaven' or 'God's abundant forgiveness'), they are prepared to accept it as the authentic teaching of Jesus. Yet when they come across something they don't like (such as 'hell', 'sexual morality' or 'the need for us to forgive others'), this is dismissed as the creation of early Christians. One of the big problems with playing fast and loose with what the Gospels actually say is that you end up creating a Jesus in your own image. It is rarely an attractive spectacle.
† The present chapter divisions in the Bible owe their origin to an early Archbishop of Canterbury, Stephen Langton, who put them into the Latin Bible in 1205.

Christ' in the Greek in which the New Testament was written: hence, rather confusingly, we talk of 'Jesus Christ' as if 'Christ' was his family name). We have written about Jesus and the Gospels in *The Life* and we refer you to that for other details. The first three Gospels are called the Synoptic Gospels (*synoptic* means they can be viewed together) and have a general similarity of outlook and style. Although the fourth Gospel, John, has a generally similar sequence of events, it is somewhat different in style. John records more of Jesus' teaching to his disciples and less of his public teaching. Interestingly enough, there are no parables in John's Gospel.

Luke's Gospel is particularly fascinating, because it is the first part of a two-book account; the second volume – the Acts of the Apostles – is 'what happened next' after the resurrection of Jesus and recounts how the church spread from Jerusalem to Rome. Although neither the text of Acts nor the Gospel bears his name, the early church was unanimous in assigning these books to the Luke who appears in Acts as a travelling companion of Paul and is mentioned in some of the letters of the New Testament.[1] There is no real reason to argue against this attribution – why would anyone invent authorship by such a minor figure when you could pretend it was written by someone much more important, such as one of the twelve disciples? There are suggestions in the earliest writers that Luke was a Gentile (a non-Jew) from that part of modern-day Syria that borders the Mediterranean. What is unarguable is that Luke's Gospel (and Acts) is written in careful and frequently rather stylish Greek. Relevant to the issue of authenticity is the fact that in the introduction to his Gospel, Luke claims to have carefully researched the facts surrounding Jesus and to have interviewed eyewitnesses. Interestingly enough, there is a period recorded in the book of Acts (probably around AD 56–7) when Paul was imprisoned in Palestine for two years. If Luke remained his companion at this time, then he might have had the opportunity to interview people who would have been present during the three or so years when Jesus taught and healed.

So when exactly was the Gospel of Luke written? Many authorities consider it to be quite late in the first century, perhaps AD 80 or so. They may well be right, but there is actually very little support for such a late date. Indeed, there are a number of strands of evidence that suggest that the book was written before AD 70. The sequel to Luke (the Acts of the Apostles) ends with Paul imprisoned in Rome around AD 64 and there is not the slightest hint that Luke knew what was going to happen to him. The simplest explanation is that Acts (and, by implication, the Gospel of Luke) was written before Paul was sentenced or released around AD 65–6. A major issue in the dating of Luke centres on the appalling events of AD 70, when, amid the most spectacular bloodshed, the Romans crushed a Jewish revolt, besieged Jerusalem and completely levelled the temple. If the Gospel had been written *after* this catastrophe, it is rather surprising that there is no reference to the biggest calamity to hit the Jewish faith for nearly seven hundred years. True, there are prophecies of war and attack on Jerusalem in Luke,[2] but the descriptions are so generalised as to suggest they were written before, rather than after, the events. (Actually, as has sometimes been pointed out, relations between the Jews and the Romans were so explosive that around AD 30 you didn't need supernatural gifting to make a guess that it was all going to end in blood and tears.)

So there seems no reason to presume a later date than AD 64 for Luke's Gospel. In fact, a little thought suggests that by this time, around thirty years after the crucifixion of Jesus, there would have been growing pressure for written accounts. By now the church had spread so widely that in some remote areas the teaching was probably based on third- or fourth-hand oral accounts ('I was taught this from Simeon, who learned it from Crispus, who himself was taught it by Peter the disciple of the Lord' – that sort of thing). It would be only natural that, around this time, church leaders would realise that creating more fixed, written accounts that could be copied and passed on was a good thing. And of course, by the AD 60s, the first generation of eyewitnesses and disciples would have been beginning to die off. Peter, very much the leader of the first generation of Christians, was executed around AD 64. Was his death the trigger for committing words to parchment?

'Fine,' we hear someone say, 'that's still a gap of three decades: perfectly long enough for someone to create the story of the Prodigal and a lot of other things too.' Maybe, but we want to suggest that there are at least four reasons why we can confidently attribute this parable to Jesus.

1. THE LOST ART OF MEMORISATION

It is entirely likely that a story like the Prodigal could have been memorised and passed on accurately by the early disciples, even without being written down. Those of us living in the fast-moving West with its constant and ever-changing bombardment of sounds and images fail to appreciate how, in more traditional cultures, memorisation is normal. This was brought home to Chris when he started lecturing in Beirut in 1980. In the absence of decent textbooks, he taught through dictation, coupled with writing out headings and key sentences on a blackboard, which his earnest students dutifully copied down. After a few weeks it was time for a test. Having been warned that because of the pressure for success (that matter of family honour!) he needed to watch out for cheating, Chris rigorously supervised the test and felt confident that he had prevented any dishonesty. Afterwards, he took the forty or so papers away and began to mark them. On the second paper he paused suddenly, struck by a terrible realisation: the answer he was reading was identical to the one he had just marked. He put it down to coincidence, only to find that the exam papers of the third and fourth students were also almost totally identical. As he marked on, it soon became appallingly apparent that on most questions there were only slight differences in the answers – an odd word changed here, a sentence restructured there. Entire blocks of text, sometimes five or six sentences long, were absolutely identical, word for word. The realisation gripped him that somehow the most outrageous form of cheating had taken place. He sought advice from the head of department, who glanced at the papers and shrugged. 'What do you expect? They've just memorised all you taught them.' And they had. Almost every student had memorised everything that Chris had written and dictated, word for word, and had been able to repeat it in the exam. In fact, when they did get textbooks, Chris had students asking him which *chapters* they needed to memorise. He began to notice students walking around campus, heads buried in books, their lips moving silently as they committed sentence after sentence to memory.

Other people have reported that similar feats of memory are perfectly ordinary in what are termed 'oral' or 'pre-literary' cultures, where written documents are rare. There can be little doubt that the earliest disciples of Jesus were quite capable of memorising an account of his life and passing it on to others with virtual word-perfect accuracy. In other words, we may have the account of the Prodigal in very much the form it was given.

2. THE FINGERPRINT OF RURAL PALESTINE

We have already commented that the world of the parables is that of rural Palestine with its sowers, fishermen and shepherds, and the language and imagery of the parables are utterly consistent with this setting.* Now, if the parables were invented, this is really rather extraordinary. Within a generation of Jesus, the leaders of the growing church were based in Greek-speaking, predominantly non-Jewish urban settlements around the northern edges of the Mediterranean. Palestine, particularly after the brutal crushing of the Jewish uprising and the destruction of the temple in AD 70, had become history. Had anyone tried to invent the parables or even rewrite them, they would not have had the knowledge to fake so flawlessly the authentic atmosphere of a rural backwater of the Roman world. In fact, they almost certainly would not have tried. After all, even one and a half thousand years later, Shakespeare, a genius if ever there was one, made no serious effort to recreate another culture; his ancient Rome or his contemporary Denmark or Italy is always recognisable as Elizabethan England.

3. THE STRANGE CASE OF THE MISSING PARABLES

In the booklist at the back you will find reference to a recently published guide to the parables for the serious student. It's the fruit of a lifetime's study by Klyne Snodgrass and is called *Stories with Intent: A Comprehensive Guide to the Parables of Jesus*. An 850-page volume with some 270 pages of fine-print endnotes, it's not light

---

* Let us give you one somewhat bizarre instance, which you will not find in any commentary. In one of his mini-parables Jesus says, 'Which of you fathers, if your son asks for a fish, will give him a snake instead?' (Luke 11:11). We find it an odd saying because we never associate fish and snakes: sea fishermen never catch snakes. Chris, who has worked in conservation in this region, points out that in the *freshwater* lakes of northern Palestine and central Lebanon, swimming snakes are extremely common near the shore and can easily be caught by accident. On its own, this proves nothing; but it is one of the many little details that point to an authentic Galilean origin for the parables.

reading. In it, however, you will find the fascinating observation that the early church did not use the sort of parables that Jesus told: parables effectively ended with the resurrection.[3] Is it believable that an organisation that didn't use parables should actually invent them for its founder?

4. THE IMPROBABILITY OF THE INVENTION OF THE PRODIGAL

Let's home in here from parables in general to this specific parable, and let's make a claim: *the creator of this parable has to be Jesus.* As justification of this apparently outrageous statement, consider the story of the Prodigal as a three-act soap opera plot.

Act 1: Younger son rebels against Dad, leaves home and, after spending his wealth recklessly, ends up in the gutter.

Act 2: Amid his misery, younger son has a moment of clarity and decides to return home. There Dad spontaneously forgives him, freely restores him to his original status and orders celebrations all round.

Act 3: Faithful elder brother – nose thoroughly put out of joint – goes ballistic with Dad. Dad rebukes elder son and justifies himself.

Put like this, do you see that this is an extraordinarily problematic tale for any organisation to promote? It is dangerously, subversively, radical. Consider what it teaches about what today we would call 'organisational loyalty'. First, it says that if someone wants to leave your organisation or community you should let the rebel go, even if it costs you money and honour. Second, it says that when it all goes pear-shaped for the rebel and he or she comes grovelling back, you are not to point out how this was an inevitable result of refusing to obey the leadership's guidance and wisdom. Instead you are to welcome the rebel back with open arms and celebration (with not so much as a word of 'told you so' or 'serve you right'). And third (even worse), the parable suggests that those loyal members who stay *within* the organisation and support all it does might actually be the ones who are in trouble. It's rather like producing a military manual suggesting that deserters should be welcomed back with a medal, or a corporate policy document which says that when company staff have taken unauthorised holidays they should be rewarded on their return with a party. No organisation could ever survive on such a teaching. Quite simply, you don't make up stories like this. You burn them and keep a wary eye on the author.*

The only reason why the early church dared to share this story is that it came from Jesus himself.

---

* If you don't believe us, then you ought to read Tertullian (*On Modesty 8: Certain General Principles of Parabolic Interpretation*). Writing as a church leader around AD 200 and faced with persecution and moral problems within his congregation, Tertullian expresses his unease about telling this parable to Christians. He felt it might encourage them to be what he calls 'tightrope walkers' on matters of morality, as it supported the 'dangerous belief' that if you fell into sin you could always be welcomed back.

3

About Parables

DEFINING PARABLES

Jesus did not invent the parable – there are a few in the Old Testament[1] and similar examples occur in other cultures – but he seems to have used parables in teaching the public with a frequency that was unusual.[2] But *why* did he use them? And, more importantly, how far are we to go in interpreting them? There are many problems to do with understanding parables, some of our own making, because in the West we do not tend to use them very much. In this chapter we want to look at what parables are and why Jesus used them so much.

One striking difficulty is the question of actually defining what a parable is. As used in the Gospels, the word *parable* seems to cover almost everything from what we would call a simple analogy or metaphor (as in 'he was as bold as a lion') to an allegory, a fully developed tale in which all the key parts have some other deeper significance.[3] Normally, though, when people think of parables they think of something that is at least a few sentences long; something that you could consider as a story, however brief. A good technical definition is that 'a parable is an expanded analogy used to convince and persuade'.[4] This is useful in that it highlights the idea of a parable as a vehicle to *give a message*. Parables are not stories to amuse: they are a method of delivering a lesson. Yet this definition overlooks one of the main characteristics of a parable, a feature hinted at by the related mathematical word, *parabola*, for a curved path or orbit. A parable is, in effect, a curved or *indirect* way of giving a message. This is something to which we will return.

Two warnings are in order here. The first is centred on the all-too-common definition of parables as being 'earthly stories with a heavenly meaning'. Not only is this too trite, it is also dangerous, for the simple reason that it implies that the parables have 'no earthly relevance'. In fact, all Jesus' parables have the very greatest earthly relevance, covering as they do the most important of all topics: how we are to relate to God and each other. Jesus' parables weren't bland ethical truisms, the first-century equivalent of Christmas-cracker mottos. Jesus was a prophet in the biblical sense: not just a man who talked about future events, but also someone who communicated God's truth to his generation. The fact that Jesus taught awkward and unpalatable truths is the reason why he ended up being opposed and, ultimately, crucified.

A second warning is necessary, because if you do any reading on the parables you will often find statements which imply that Jesus was a 'simple peasant'. That ambivalent and loaded word 'simple' is now sometimes merely hinted at, but the notion lingers. The idea seems to be of some weather-beaten village rustic, pulling the straw out of his mouth and uttering (with a suitably uncouth accent) some rough-hewn gem of wisdom. This is, in effect, intellectual snobbery. Of course Jesus came from a rural culture, but let's not be so condescending as to think that *rural* equals *primitive* or even *stupid*. Consider what may seem an utterly irrelevant question: when the sun set and the pitch darkness of night descended on them, how did the occupants of Nazareth busy themselves? The answer is surely that they did what most human beings did before books, gaslight, electricity, radio and television. They sat around a fire in the flickering darkness and talked and sang together for hours. They would have made up and recounted tales, quoted passages of Scripture, passed on genealogies, created and refined poetry and sung songs. Such oral cultures leave little behind them because their achievements are so rarely preserved; yet they develop and celebrate the very highest levels of verbal skills. Talk to any Westerner who has spent time in such a society, and they will often tell you how embarrassed they were when their hosts turned to them and said, 'Now *you* sing us a song,' or, 'Tell us one of *your* tales.' For all our technical abilities, you may be sure that when it comes to skills of memorisation, storytelling and general dexterity with words, such people are the ones who are superior.

Incidentally, a related characteristic of Jesus' parables is the way that they are set in a normal world. Unlike, say, the fables of Aesop, here there are no talking animals, no bizarre events, not even any magic. We are a long way from Hogwarts or even Narnia. There is wisdom here: the most effective parables are no doubt those that are set as closely as possible to the world in which the hearers live. Talking of science fiction, C. S. Lewis writes, 'To tell of how odd things struck odd people is to have an oddity too much.'[5] That rule applies to parables: too much novelty can actually be counterproductive. The world of the Prodigal was not far removed at all from that of those who heard the tale. That's why it cut so deep.

THE RATIONALE OF PARABLES

So why did Jesus use parables? We suggest three reasons, which we can label as follows: to appeal, reveal, conceal.

1. Parables appeal

It is clear in the Gospels that Jesus found himself surrounded by crowds, often to the point that he had to go to considerable trouble to discourage them.[6] There was evidently something about his teaching that people found attractive. Part of that attractiveness was the fresh, authoritative way that he taught compared to other religious teachers.[7] Nevertheless, the fact that he taught in parables was obviously a factor. The parables clearly had an *appeal* in at least three senses of the word.

First of all, they had an appeal because they were attractive stories that people enjoyed hearing. This shouldn't really surprise us: in John's Gospel Jesus is given the title of 'the Word' of God and – not surprisingly – the Word made flesh was good with words. We have not lost our appetite for good use of language. There are many television or radio celebrities who, although they may have very little that is novel or important to say, can keep you listening because you know they can be guaranteed to come up with some striking way of saying it. Earlier we spoke of parables being 'curved ways of giving a message' and this is very relevant here. One of the problems of teaching spiritual truths is that there is not a great deal of scope for novelty in what you teach. After all, as has been wisely said, people do not so much need to be taught as reminded. So, to avoid boring people by repetition, if you can't vary *what* you teach, you ought at least to vary *how* you teach. By giving a message that took a curved, fresh path to his hearers, Jesus defied boredom and ensured freshness. The way that Jesus structured at least some of his teaching as parables would also have allowed it to be transmitted easily. The parables lodge indelibly in the mind and so can easily be passed on. To use the modern phrase, there was something 'viral' about them; you can imagine someone going back to the village and saying, 'Listen to what I heard Jesus of Nazareth say . . .' So in this sense you could say that the parables were appealing. There are, of course, lessons here for how Christians present their teaching today.

The parables, however, made an appeal in a second sense. Jesus was clearly not someone who told interesting stories just because they kept people happy. The parables are all clearly intended to provoke a response from the hearers. To take the Parable of the

Prodigal, you can imagine Jesus gazing around the audience as he told it, inviting them by his look and tone to give *their* judgement on what the father should have done. The parables are like a lawyer's appeal in court; they are a petition for a verdict. It is no coincidence that some of our most successful television shows today are those where the audience can phone in with their verdict. If you are involved in a story, you cannot ignore it. So in these parables Jesus effectively stops and says (sometimes literally), 'Now, what do *you* think?' or, 'What's *your* verdict?'[8] Here, too, there are no doubt lessons for us in communication. This is one reason why children's talks in church are often more memorable than the adult sermon that follows. When we talk to children we seek involvement, a process that we often ignore with adults.

There is a final sense in which the parables appeal: they make a call to commitment. Parables acted as the great filtering mechanism for Jesus' audiences. Some of his hearers no doubt shook their heads, shrugged their shoulders and walked away, never to be seen again. Others apparently found themselves compelled and intrigued by what they heard and puzzled over it. Some of them probably returned later to Jesus for private conversations with him, seeking what 'The Prodigal' or 'The Hidden Treasure' or 'The Mustard Seed' meant for them personally. A passage in Mark seems to suggest that in this sharply divided response, Jesus saw the fulfilment of prophecy that not all of God's people would respond to God's message because some had already closed their minds to the truth.[9] Their failure to respond to the appeal of the parables showed that they had already rejected God.

2. Parables reveal

Parables, then, appeal in every sense of the word. But they also *reveal*. The parables are not tales for amusement and bemusement, but for enlightenment. Jesus was not seeking a round of applause, but rather thought and involvement. Some of the parables seem intended to have the audience walking away frowning and shaking their heads in puzzled anger.

Here we come to one of the key things about a parable being 'indirect'. The longer parables in particular invite us into their world; we get sucked into the story and we see things from the perspective of those within the parable. Then, as the punchline is delivered, we realise that the figure we are gazing at is ourselves. As with a mirror, we see ourselves in a way that is very different from what we had imagined. This is important; it is amazing how rarely human beings welcome news of who – or what – they really are. As most of us know from experience, a direct challenge to someone can often be remarkably ineffective. The moment the words strike, the barriers drop down and our words are deflected away. You can almost hear them say quietly to themselves, 'He's not talking about me,' or, 'She always says that sort of thing, but she doesn't really mean it.'

Sometimes the defences can be very strong: anyone who has been involved in speaking in something like a church setting will have come across the following situation. You have given a talk with what you feel certain was considerable power and sharpness on some evil and the necessity of dealing with it. As you stand at the door, shaking hands, you wait for the response of the challenged or offended soul. Instead, what you get is something like this: 'I really want to thank you for your message; I can't believe how well you described someone I know.' Total deflection has been achieved. Our defences against being personally challenged are so impenetrable that something other than a direct attack is often required. It is here that a parable can work wonders. Like a stealth bomber, it sneaks through the defences undetected and unopposed and delivers its weaponry on the target. Through the parables, Jesus was able to speak truths that would otherwise have been filtered out before they could be considered.

We need to reflect on the difficulty of revealing reality to people. The nature of the problem is shown up in those series of comparisons that you often hear people jokingly use. You know the sort of thing: '*I* am sensitive, *you* are troubled, *he* is neurotic,' or, '*I* carefully manage my finances, *you* save every penny, *she* is mean.' The point of these comparisons is that a fault we see clearly in others may either be invisible in ourselves or even recognised as a virtue. In his poem 'The Louse', Robert Burns says this: 'O wad some Power the giftie gie us, To see oursels as ithers see us!' The trick with parables is that they can do just that.

If you have ever looked carefully at the helmet of some ancient suit of armour, you will have realised that the wearer would only have had a very limited view of the world; reality would have been contracted to a slit. The reality is that many of us have created a psychological equivalent and live out our existence inside it; we stumble on through life utterly oblivious to everything outside this narrow field of view. This psychological tunnel vision allows us to ignore utterly what we do not wish to see about ourselves and our relationships with others. Parables take the helmet off.

Let's take another illustration. We all like photographs. Yet to see photographs of an occasion at which you were present is often somewhat disconcerting. There is a different, new perspective; you see yourself as others see you. You sense yourself frowning: *I shouldn't have worn that suit; I ought to lose some weight; I had no idea that haircut looked like that* . . . Parables are like such photographs, and sometimes they are just as uncomfortable. And interestingly, the first person we look at in a photograph is ourselves!

One of the challenges of parables, then, is how they reveal to us who we really are.

3. Parables conceal

We can no doubt easily understand both the need to appeal and the need to reveal. But to *conceal*? That may not fit with our image of Jesus. Yet the Bible is clear that there was something about the parables that involved making things obscure. So Mark says this of Jesus' teaching to the public: 'With many similar parables Jesus spoke the word to them, as much as they could understand. He did not say anything to them without using a parable. But when he was alone with his own disciples, he explained everything.'[10]

Let's try to explain what's going on here. Part of the issue is no doubt the shame and honour culture. In a culture in which a public rebuke is a mortal offence, it is often easier to tell a parable which, with its parabolic flight path, allows the words to strike home without the insult of the direct accusation. Anyone working in such a shame and honour culture soon learns to be very attentive to stories that people tell them. As often as not, there is a message behind the words. So if, soon after starting a programme of corporate reorganisation, a new manager begins to hear stories of the unfortunate fate of a predecessor who tried to change the status quo, then he or she needs to watch him- or herself. A disguised criticism is no less serious for being hidden.

Yet there is almost certainly more than that. Most of us reading this will take for granted what it means to live in what is (for the most part) a democratic and peaceful society. In the West we pride ourselves on our freedom to say what we want. (In fact, you could argue that this is one of our problems.) Yet there are many cultures where you must not only think twice before you open your mouth, but look over your shoulder as well. In the troubled and simmering Palestine around AD 30, there were more forces to which Jesus would have paid attention. To the Romans, Jesus would already have been known as John the Baptist's successor and his name was probably already down on some scroll of potential troublemakers. The Jews had a history of almost perpetual rebellion against occupying armies and the Romans kept an anxious watch for any spark that might signal an outbreak of some new uprising. In particular they were concerned lest any radical preacher might arise who would become the focus of the great Jewish hope of a God-ordained deliverer – the Messiah. For us the little phrase 'kingdom of God' is cosy spiritual language; for the Romans it would have been something very dangerously different: after all, a kingdom implies a king. The ambiguous language of the parables allowed Jesus to talk about the kingdom without directly arousing Roman suspicion.

Yet it was not just the Romans who were uneasy about the Messiah. Many elements within the Jewish faith had acquired status and possessions that they did not wish to see challenged. The Pharisees saw themselves as guardians of the faith. The Sadducees and others had a very strong investment in the temple, with its exclusive franchise on what has always been that most profitable of religious businesses: the forgiveness of sins. They too would have had their concerns about a radical preacher from Galilee who seemed to be offering an alternative forgiveness. These potential enemies, both outside and inside the Jewish faith, meant that it would have been easy, through a careless word or an explicit claim, for Jesus to have been executed very quickly or put in prison. Parables, with their ambiguous, oblique way of stating things, offer a way of challenging people while minimising the risk to yourself.

Chris was once the victim of exactly this sort of thing in Beirut. He had just given an important exam when a student walked up to him, smiled and said with a quiet, polite firmness, 'Sir, did you hear about the chemistry professor who failed a student and had his car blown up?' As the student walked away, Chris was very uncomfortably aware of being on the wrong end of a parable. It was, he presumed, a threat. Yet if it was a threat, it was one he could do nothing about. If it had been a note with a message scrawled on it – 'Pass me, Prof, or your car gets it' – then the threat would have been clear and action could have been taken. But as it was, it was simply too ambiguous.* As we will see in the Parable

* As it happened, the student passed without needing any 'help'. But Chris checked under his car for a few days anyway. That's the thing about parables: you can't be too careful with them.

of the Prodigal, there are allegations made in it against the Pharisees, but they are elusive and too vague to form the basis of any action. The Pharisees would have known that Jesus was getting at them and it would have annoyed them, but there wasn't much they could do about it. The power of imprisonment and execution lay in the hands of the Romans and it was going to need something far more than indirect and veiled criticism to get them to act. (You can imagine the conversation in the governor's palace, can't you? 'You say he threatened you? How?' 'Well, your Excellency, you see, he . . . told stories . . .')

It is significant that parables, often told with a wink or a nod, have always flourished under totalitarian regimes. The literature of Eastern Europe under communism is full of them. Sometimes truth is too dangerous to speak unless you disguise it.

So was Jesus trying to save his life by using parables? Almost certainly something more complex was going on. We presume that Jesus knew by now that he was going to have to die. Yet he clearly also knew that there were things that had to be done first. He had to teach and proclaim the good news of the kingdom of God so that Israel, God's people, would have the opportunity either to accept or to reject him. He also had to call and train those who would be the nucleus of a new people of God – the twelve who were his closest disciples. To do both these things Jesus could afford neither protracted arrest nor premature execution. The result is what we see in the Gospels: a Jesus who was clearly prepared to go to the cross, but on his own timetable and not that of the Romans or the religious authorities. If we try to trace Jesus' travels, we see him using Palestine's tangled politics to evade arrest by crossing from one ruler's area of control to that of another. The parables are the verbal equivalent of this dodging and weaving. In a situation where his every word was scrutinised, they allowed Jesus both to proclaim and to conceal his own identity. It is significant that during the final weeks of Jesus' ministry, his parables become much more confrontational and are accompanied by much more explicit statements. By now the time for subtle concealment and evasion was over.

'What is a parable?' we asked. Let's conclude our discussion with a mini-parable of our own. A parable is a message with clothes on. And as clothes appeal, reveal and conceal that which lies underneath, so do parables.

THE INTERPRETATION OF PARABLES

Finally in this chapter, let's consider how we interpret parables. Most people would agree that, in considering any passage in the Bible, you have to do your best to interpret the text faithfully. Yet this is not always as easy as it sounds. The very nature of parables means that some degree of response by the hearer is required. The fact that even one of the longer parables such as the Prodigal is still little more than a skeleton of a tale means that we are expected to add flesh to it ourselves. A response is invited – that's the point! Nevertheless, in making a response, two dangers are present. One is to distort the parable by omitting what it says, by deliberately or accidentally overlooking what is clearly present. The other – you guessed it – is to distort the parable by adding to it, by creating details that are not present. We must neither under-read nor over-read the text.

A central and contested issue here is the extent to which the details in a parable have a meaning. So, for instance, in the early centuries of Christianity the tendency grew up to see parables as allegories; as tales in which almost everything has meaning. Sometimes this reached a point where, frankly, the whole practice became rather silly. When some preachers taught the Parable of the Prodigal, for example, their congregations were told that the fatted calf symbolised Jesus (because it was slain). The result of such an approach was that sermons on the parables became more a testimony to the ingenuity and imagination of the preacher than anything else. In the last century, there has been a reaction away from this to a view in which a parable is seen as having only one single, simple point. However, as is so often the case, the swing of the pendulum may have gone too far. In the parable that is the key to all the parables, that of the Sower (perhaps better titled the 'Parable of the Four Soils'),[11] we are given the interpretation by Jesus. In this we are told that all the key elements of the parable have separate and distinct meanings: in other words, this parable is an allegory. The reality is that because, as we have seen, parables vary so much in their style, we simply cannot generalise: they may have a single meaning or many lessons. What is important is that we do not strain the interpretation to put in a meaning that neither Jesus nor his hearers would recognise. As we will see with the Parable of the Prodigal, there is a single theme to the story; nevertheless, the three central figures all show us slightly different aspects of that theme.

4

The Setting of the Parable of the Prodigal

Before we consider the three acts of the Parable of the Prodigal, let's look at the setting. The parable was not given in a vacuum, but rather it was a response to a particular issue. It is always a good idea to try to set passages of the Bible in their context, and this is no exception. The Parable of the Prodigal is the third of three parables, all of which centre around 'being lost'. They form something of the central piece of Luke's Gospel and some have argued that this is not accidental; a major theme in Luke is of Jesus 'redeeming' or 'rescuing' the lost. If this is the case, then what we have here is, in a very literal sense, the core of the gospel as Luke saw it.

Fortunately, we do not have to guess too much about the precise context in which Jesus taught this parable; the background is given by two verses at the beginning of Luke 15: 'Now the tax collectors and sinners were all gathering around to hear Jesus. But the Pharisees and the teachers of the law muttered, "This man welcomes sinners and eats with them."' The background is the grumbling of the Pharisees, and here we need to think a little bit about who they were and what they stood for.

THE PHARISEES

Consider the setting. In Jesus' time, the Jewish religion faced twin enemies.* There was the blatant threat of extinction by extermination from the thuggish and predatory Roman occupation, and the more subtle (but no less dangerous) threat of extinction by contamination from the ever more popular Greek culture. The Greek way of life no doubt aroused the same emotions amongst the Jews of Palestine at this time as Westernisation evokes in the Middle East today – namely, bitterness and rage among the faithful as they see their very world dissolve around them. There were various responses to these twin threats, but one of the most important was that of the Pharisees and their allies, the 'teachers of the law'. Their answer focused on enforcing religious purity by imposing on the faithful a very long list of those things they must do and an equally long list of things they mustn't do. The Pharisees, focused around the temple in Jerusalem, were essentially social enforcers trying to ensure that the community was singing not just from the same hymn sheet, but from the *right* hymn sheet.

To help us understand the Pharisees, imagine a society where religion controls everything. Anyone who has lived in the Middle East will be familiar with this sort of culture within Islam, but there have been parallel movements within almost every branch of Christianity and Judaism. In such settings there are always men† who feel it is their divine calling to make sure that everybody does what is truly right. Such people have a great deal of authority and they tend to use it. With a single stony glance they

---

* We have covered this and other aspects of the background to the Gospels in *The Life*.

† They *are* always men, and although they tend to be negative about women, it is surprising how useful they find female support in helping to impose their codes of righteousness.

can scatter children playing outside a place of worship; with the merest scowl at a hemline they can make the most determined woman retreat hastily indoors; and with the flicker of a cold frown they can turn the noisy frivolity of a social gathering to silence. Such 'Pharisees' not only miss nothing, but they make sure that everybody knows that they miss nothing. Their *raison d'être* is religion, but actually they are far more interested in behaviour than belief. Indeed, there is much about them that is reminiscent of the unlamented secret police of Eastern Europe's communism. It is doubtless unwelcome to believers of a Dawkinsian creed that atheism has its Pharisees too, but there really is precious little difference between imposing correct religious practices and ensuring party solidarity. Political Correctness likewise has its Pharisees, who are all too zealous in instructing us on what we should and should not say.

It used to be traditional to say that the big difference between Jesus and the Pharisees (and the Jewish faith generally) was that, while Jesus taught what we might term 'salvation by grace' (that is, you get into heaven because God freely forgives you), they taught what we term 'salvation by works' (that is, you get into heaven because you have earned a place by your good deeds). Some interpreters have gone even further by linking this with the Old and New Testaments. To them, the Pharisees represent the Old Testament way of doing things, where a God of judgement and wrath is placated by sacrifices and good works, while Jesus represents the New Testament's system of a God of love and mercy who saves by grace. Unfortunately, to take this view is to distort the Old Testament and probably the Pharisees too. Consider this great expression: 'But you are a forgiving God, gracious and compassionate, slow to anger and abounding in love.' While it sounds like the essence of the New Testament, it actually occurs in the Old Testament. Not only so, but that phrase (or something very close to it) occurs eight times.[1] The reality is that the differences between the Testaments have been exaggerated. In fact, if you read Jesus' criticism of the Pharisees carefully, you will see that what he blamed them for was not the fact that they were stuck in the Old Testament, but rather that they hadn't got stuck into it enough. It is probably the case that the Pharisees and the other Jewish teachers did actually believe that God had saved his people by grace. The problem was that they believed in grace *in theory*, but in works *in practice*. You wouldn't have to search too far in Christian communities to find those who have preached God's free forgiveness from the pulpit while enforcing the most judgemental rules of conduct in life. In fact, living by grace is actually quite challenging; it is far easier to slip back into the human race's default mode of trying to please God by doing good things.

In summary, there was much that was good in the Pharisees, but it was flawed. It is an old, sad rule that religion when it goes rotten goes badly rotten. The Pharisees no doubt meant well, but in their anxiety to create a pure and holy society they created a harsh and judgemental system. They may have been sincere, but they were sincerely wrong. They were, to use Mark Twain's pungent phrase, 'good men in the worst sense of the word'. They created an exclusive club with benefits to those inside and condemnation for those outside. The severity and all-embracing nature of the Pharisees' version of Judaism meant that lots of people could not keep to it. The result was an entire class of people to whom the Pharisees gave the shorthand term of *sinners*. (Some Bible versions put the term in quotation marks: 'sinners'; in this context they are probably correct.) This general group of 'moral underachievers' are often linked with a group of specific failures: the tax collectors. The problem with the tax collectors that made them the focus of explicit contempt was not that they were working for the first-century equivalent of the Inland Revenue; it was that they were collecting money for the Romans. It is one of the unpleasant characteristics of occupying armies that they tend not simply to bully you, but also to charge you for the privilege. In the Palestine of AD 30, strict Jews found this even more unpleasant, because the fact that they worked for the Gentile Romans meant that tax collectors were inevitably infected by their paymasters' moral uncleanliness. Being ritually unclean was, in effect, a communicable disease.

We are told that the precise focus of the trouble between the Pharisees and Jesus was meal fellowship. This again is something that we have rather overlooked with our habit of staggered microwave meals round the TV and the whole 'excuse-me-while-I-grab-a-bite' sort of thing. In the culture of the Gospels (and it is still true today in the Middle East), a meal is not just food; it is a community event that creates and cements social obligations. For you to eat with someone else is for you to accept them as a social and even moral equal. You do not eat with those you condemn or those you see as enemies. So when Jesus ate with these so-called 'sinners', he was saying to all that he accepted them. It is probably worthwhile making the point that the people at issue were those who had either repented of their past life or were doing their best to make a break with it. No allegations have come down to us that Jesus himself engaged in sinful behaviour. (If he had, then the clumsy business of finding an excuse to have him executed that all the Gospels record could have been avoided.) The issue was that these 'moral failures', as we might call them, either could not, or would not, meet the Pharisees' code of righteous behaviour.

It is quite likely that the Pharisees objected to Jesus eating with those whom they considered outcasts for several reasons. One would have been that his action was an all too public rebuke to their authority and an open rejection of their religious code. Another would have been that they saw Jesus as offering God's pardon outside the monopoly on forgiveness that they controlled through the temple. One other would have been their frustration that, after all their work on creating a holy wall of exclusion between the righteous (themselves) and the 'sinners' (everyone else), Jesus was knocking it down. No doubt the Pharisees saw Jewish society as already sliding down a very slippery slope and they would have felt that Jesus was greasing it. He was a very dangerous man.

Significantly, what seems to have exasperated Jesus was not the Pharisees' rulings as such, but their mean-spirited nature. When they should have celebrated, they were sour and miserable. They loved grumbling and muttering; they were very positive about negatives. That is worth noticing: as a formal religious movement the Pharisees are long dead, but their chilling killjoy spirit lives on.

A careful reading of the Gospels suggests that the opposition between Jesus and the religious authorities occurred in three phases. The first phase was marked by a probing and increasing curiosity on the part of the authorities as they nervously asked, 'Who is this man? What is he saying? Is he a threat to us?' Jesus responded with both veiled claims about himself and challenges to his questioners that confirmed their worst suspicions. The second phase saw the curiosity replaced by a growing and ever more belligerent hostility. In response, Jesus seems to have been unbending but defensive. It is in this phase that the Parable of the Prodigal occurs. The third phase, essentially the last few months or so of his ministry, was marked by a blatant hostility on the part of the Pharisees that is evidenced by trick questions designed to provoke the Roman authorities into executing Jesus. In the Parable of the Prodigal, this final phase of confrontation is already looming on the horizon, yet a final, irrevocable breach between Jesus and the Pharisees has not yet occurred. In the parables of Luke 15, we sense that Jesus is still trying to persuade his opponents to see things his way.

THE PRECURSOR PARABLES

Jesus, then, is faced with muttering by the religious establishment and he responds with three parables, which for the sake of convenience may be called here the 'Lost Sheep', the 'Lost Coin' and the 'Lost Son' (or is it 'Lost *Sons*'?). It is easy to see these as variants on a theme, yet each has a slightly different emphasis. We need to look at these precursors briefly.

The Lost Sheep
The text of this parable reads:

> Now the tax collectors and sinners were all gathering around to hear Jesus. But the Pharisees and the teachers of the law muttered, 'This man welcomes sinners and eats with them.'
>
> Then Jesus told them this parable: 'Suppose one of you has a hundred sheep and loses one of them. Doesn't he leave the ninety-nine in the open country and go after the lost sheep until he finds it? And when he finds it, he joyfully puts it on his shoulders and goes home. Then he calls his friends and neighbours together and says, "Rejoice with me; I have found my lost sheep." I tell you that in the same way there will be more rejoicing in heaven over one sinner who repents than over ninety-nine righteous persons who do not need to repent.'
>
> (Luke 15:1–7)

It may be significant that Luke writes that Jesus told them this *parable* in the singular. Was he perhaps referring to what we consider as three separate parables as one? The very loose nature of the Greek word translated 'parable' might allow for this. Certainly all three parables in Luke 15 are very strongly linked and build to a finale.

The Parable of the Lost Sheep focuses on the figure of the shepherd who has lost one of his flock. Leaving the rest (presumably with one or more under-shepherds; a hundred sheep would be a very large flock for a single shepherd), he goes out and searches for the lost sheep, finds it and carries it back to the others. At this point (as is often the case in parables), reality becomes slightly exaggerated and there is a celebratory party. Most parables have a punchline and here (introduced with the phrase 'I tell you that in the same way . . .') Jesus says that heaven (probably a reverent short-hand for God) rejoices more over repentant sinners than over those 'who need not repent'. (This last comment is presumably ironic or even sarcastic; no one knew better than Jesus that we all need to repent. Remember that line, 'Let any one of you who is without sin be the first to throw a stone'?[2])

The clear emphasis of the parable is on two things: the lost need to be sought, and when they are found, joyful celebration is appro-priate. In the face of the grumbling over his meeting with sinners, Jesus says that true faith should rejoice when the lost return safely.

There are some features of this parable that should be noticed. By referring to 'one sinner who repents', Jesus is pointing out that he has not assumed that sin does not matter: as we noted above, those with whom he eats are *repentant* sinners. It is far from easy to balance a willingness to accept those who have turned from sin with the necessity of keeping the appropriate distance from those who continue in it. Sad to report, the Christian Church has found it all too easy to criticise those who, in reaching out, overreach.

One oddity in the text should make us think. Addressing the Pharisees and teachers of the law, Jesus says, 'Suppose one of you has a hundred sheep and loses one of them.' At first glance this is slightly curious: while no one is really certain whether shepherds were despised, as manual labourers they would have been a long way below the Pharisees on the social ladder. So why does Jesus treat his audience as if they are shepherds? The answer may be that he is alluding to what would have been a well-known Old Testament passage. In Ezekiel 34, there is a prophecy against the 'shepherds of Israel' for their failure to look after the flock. It is too long a passage to quote in its entirety, but one well worth reading. It begins with a clear and strong denunciation by God of 'the shepherds of Israel' who have neglected in every way to look after the flock, so that 'my sheep wandered over all the mountains and on every high hill. They were scattered over the whole earth, and no one searched or looked for them.' The subject of the prophecy is clearly not agriculture, but rather the care of God's people.

The idea of a king being the shepherd was a familiar one in the Jewish faith: had not the greatest of all kings, David, literally been one? Indeed, God uses shepherd language of himself in the Old Testament.[3] If this is the case, and it seems likely, the slightly odd reference to the shepherd having *lost* the sheep may be a veiled accusation against the Pharisees. They had set themselves up as the shepherds of Israel, but the sheep had gone astray; they were those who had not so much lost the plot as lost the flock. There may be more: for those 'with ears to hear', Jesus may actually have been making a claim about himself as the shepherd who had come to rescue the sheep. Given that in Ezekiel the shepherd is God, this is a most serious claim. Such a position is strengthened by the fact that Jesus calls himself 'the good shepherd' in John's Gospel.[4] (Incidentally, this makes the point that many of the titles that Jesus takes to himself and which we take for granted are those which his contemporaries would have seen as belonging to God alone.)

The Lost Coin

Or suppose a woman has ten silver coins and loses one. Doesn't she light a lamp, sweep the house and search carefully until she finds it? And when she finds it, she calls her friends and neighbours together and says, 'Rejoice with me; I have found my lost coin.' In the same way, I tell you, there is rejoicing in

the presence of the angels of God over one sinner who repents.
(Luke 15:8–10)

The broad emphasis of the Parable of the Lost Coin is similar to that of the previous parable. Something that is valuable has been lost; it is searched for and, when it is found, rejoicing is in order. One major difference is that – rather daringly for this culture – the central figure is female and she is shown energetically seeking the lost coin. This is one of many Bible passages that have suffered from the efforts of well-meaning interpreters who have added embellishments to the plain sense of the text. The suggestion that the coin was part of a woman's bridal headdress (as portrayed in a thousand illustrated Bible editions) is one such unnecessary elaboration. The text suggests no more than the fact that this coin was one tenth of the woman's wealth. (Although there are some disagreements, it is likely that the coin – a drachma – would have been equivalent to a day or two's wages.)

The emphasis of this parable falls on two areas. First, it highlights the priority the woman places on finding the lost coin: she lights a lamp to lift the darkness in the tiny house, sweeps the floor and searches carefully.* Second, as with the first parable, communal rejoicing is the appropriate response. The similarities are heightened by an almost identical punchline: 'In the same way, I tell you, there is rejoicing in the presence of the angels of God over one sinner who repents.'

So far, Jesus has stated that the lost should be sought and has twice emphasised the need for rejoicing over the returnees. He now offers a third parable.

---

* As a geologist, Chris rather likes the suggestion by Ken Bailey that the house was one of those typical of the Capernaum area, where the gloom created by an absence of windows was heightened by the blackness of the basalt used as the building stone.

5

The Prodigal: Act One –
The Rebellion and Ruin
of the Younger Son

We now move on to the Parable of the Prodigal. The lost-found-rejoicing themes we have seen earlier are here, but everything is heightened. The first two parables dealt with what was, in effect, lost property. This is much more serious: that most precious of things, a *son*, is lost. That we are at the culmination of a sequence is emphasised by the cold mathematics of the parables: first, one out of a hundred sheep is lost, then one out of ten coins, and now one out of two sons. The stakes are now much higher. Dispassionately put, we might handle a 1 per cent or even a 10 per cent loss, but who could bear to lose 50 per cent?

Before we look at the parable in detail it's worth noting that, although in some passages of the Bible issues (generally minor) arise depending on how the words are translated from the original languages, there are very few variations of translation in this parable. The story reads very much the same whichever Bible version you use.

> Jesus continued: 'There was a man who had two sons. The younger one said to his father, "Father, give me my share of the estate." So he divided his property between them.
>
> 'Not long after that, the younger son got together all he had, set off for a distant country and there squandered his wealth in

wild living. After he had spent everything, there was a severe famine in that whole country, and he began to be in need. So he went and hired himself out to a citizen of that country, who sent him to his fields to feed pigs. He longed to fill his stomach with the pods that the pigs were eating, but no one gave him anything.'

(Luke 15:11–16)

At first glance this is a straightforward account of the rebellion of a son and how things go badly wrong for him. Yet with such a skeletal account, the details are worth noticing.

For a start, the opening words of this parable tell us that it is not just about the younger son, but about *both* sons. Some people have assumed that the story of the second son is an addition that, like some badly built house extension, ruins an otherwise pleasing original structure. Some preachers, who would never dare assume that the matter of the elder son was an inauthentic addition, nevertheless truncate the story by majoring only on the younger son. Yet the reality that there are *two* sons is central to this parable and to be faithful to it requires that we take both into account. Nevertheless, the younger son dominates the 'first act' of the account.

We may presume that this younger son is indeed young: most Jewish men at this time would have married by twenty, so if we put him as being in his late teens we are probably not far wrong. Indeed, we may not be going too far amiss in considering him as 'the lad'. There are hints that the father's estate is considerable; he has hired servants and his lands are large enough that the elder son can be out of earshot of the rapturous homecoming. We may assume, too, that this is meant to be set in Galilee or at least somewhere in the Jewish part of Palestine. You will not be surprised to know that no one seems to have felt it worthwhile to preserve details of first-century Jewish property law for posterity, but it does seem that an elder son would receive twice as much as the other sons,[1] and that a father could distribute his wealth during his lifetime if he wished. So there does not appear to be anything illegal going on.

The actual issue at the heart of the son's request for his inheritance is not that of illegality, but something else. Most hearers of this parable, whatever their culture, have always assumed that the younger son is behaving badly. Two thousand years on, we cannot fail to detect, in the way he demands his share of the inheritance, an aggressive, testosterone-rich insolence. We may even be aware that in a Jewish society that held to the Ten Commandments, holding your father (and mother) in respect was vital. The fifth Commandment reads, 'Honour your father and your mother, as the LORD your God has commanded you, so that you may live long and that it may go well with you in the land the LORD your God is giving you.'[2]

No one has ever doubted that the son is behaving badly – yet it seems that in the modern West we have probably failed to realise exactly *how* badly. Something of the social setting underlying this parable has been made clear by the work of Ken Bailey, a missionary and theologian who lived for many years in Egypt and Lebanon and had an in-depth knowledge of the culture of the Middle East. As it happens, Chris knew him fairly well in the early 1980s, as Ken used to be a regular guest preacher at the church Chris attended in Beirut.* What Ken did was to point out the

---

* At this time the long-running Lebanese Civil War was still going on and University Baptist Church was a mere fifteen minutes' walk away from where people were engaged in trying to kill each other. Operating in a converted brothel, it was multicultural, multilingual and – unsurprisingly – multi-problem. It was perfectly common to hear the rumble of shellfire during a service, to have stray gunmen wander in and to face such everyday pastoral issues as whether or not mercenaries should be allowed to take Communion. Despite the setting, Ken, a warm and gracious man, retained a university lecturer's commitment to transmitting knowledge and it was not unknown for him to pass around lecture handouts at the start of a sermon. Any temptation to find the often slightly surreal atmosphere of worship at UBC amusing was tempered by the sobering prospect that you couldn't guarantee that either you or anybody else would still be around – or even alive – the following Sunday.

overlooked significance of matters of honour and shame and family relationships that are implied in the parable. Ken has written several books on the subject and we list some of the most relevant at the end.

Central to what *is* going on is the fact that, where a society is based around the family, for a son to ask for his inheritance is for him to strike a blow at all that his family stands for. After all, the normal pattern would have been that, as the father became elderly and infirm, the sons would have taken over the family estate and looked after him. For a younger son to demand his share was in effect to say to his father, 'I want out of this arrangement. I don't care about your welfare and I don't care the slightest about the family estate.' He would be publicly spitting in the face of his heritage, his blood ties and everything that his culture stood for. It might not be going too far to suggest that, by demanding his inheritance while the father was still alive, the son was implying that he wished his father dead.

In a first-century Jewish context, it would also have been blameworthy for the son to turn his back on the land as his heritage from the Lord God. (It was, after all, the land promised by God to his people Israel.) Notice, too, that the son seems to have sold the property rapidly. In a culture where bargaining can stretch on for hours or days, to have sold the family's estate rapidly suggests that he would have made a substantial loss. You can see the hearers of this parable shaking their heads and hear them mutter, 'Not only did this kid sell off his part of the family heritage, he didn't even get a good price for it!'

Some commentators on this parable, drawing from parallels within some branches of the Jewish faith, have considered that there might have been a formal ceremony to pronounce the son dead. Frankly, we do not know whether this is the case and it is probably pushing the evidence too far. Nevertheless, the fact that at the end of the parable the father twice refers to the younger son as having been dead and now being alive (vv. 24, 32) suggests that whether or not there was a formal ceremony, he was effectively considered to be dead. Given the fact that a parable is generally stripped down to its bare essentials, it is a good rule that when you see the repetition of a phrase, you pay attention to it.

As we follow the son, we see a progressive descent. He goes to 'a distant country'. This would have told Jesus' readers that the Prodigal had gone to the Gentiles. This in itself was not particularly worthy of criticism. After all, there was a sizeable Jewish community – the Diaspora – spread around the Mediterranean and even in what is now modern-day Iran and Iraq. Yet there is probably a subtle point here: having turned his back on his earthly father and his own land, the Prodigal has now turned his back on God and the Promised Land of his forefathers.

Jesus' hearers would have had all their worst suspicions confirmed by the account of what happened next. In one of the many tiny but masterly brushstrokes that make up the portrait of the Prodigal, we read that in this foreign land he 'squandered his wealth in wild living'. In this sort of culture, to leave home to seek one's fortune abroad is a respectable action. To return home having made a fortune is utterly praiseworthy and something that confers enormous honour on both family and community. Yet nothing of this sort happens here; on the contrary, the Prodigal's wealth trickles away like water through open fingers in what is delicately described as 'wild living'. The Greek term here may mean sexual immorality, but it may simply refer to spendthrift living or an excessive, carefree lifestyle. The traditional Jewish attitudes to finance (grotesquely and tragically caricatured by anti-Semitism) have always praised cautious financial activity, with skilful trading and careful accounting. Here we see the very opposite: no prudent, astute investment, but instead a reckless wasting of the wealth of his family. He throws it all away. At this point, Jesus' hearers must have been certain that this was a tale that could only end in disaster for the Prodigal. They were both right and wrong.

The son's rebellion and careless abuse of family resources bring their inevitable penalty with them. He exhausts his own resources and now, as famine looms, finds himself in trouble. Famines were regular occurrences in the ancient world and in societies without health services and national insurance it was always the mark of a prudent and wise manager to have resources available for hard times. Yet when disaster strikes, the Prodigal finds himself with no resources and now, as the storm clouds gather, there is no hint of any of the 'fair-weather' companions of his days of wild living. He is obliged to hire himself out to a citizen of the country. In other words, he is to become a servant of a Gentile and as the misery gathers about him, he is sent out into the country to feed pigs where his hunger is such that even the swine food looks attractive. You can imagine the shudders and expressions of disgust from those in the crowd; you didn't need to be a Pharisee to know that *that* wasn't a kosher trade.

In fact, this far in the first hearing of the story, many of the crowd would have found it extremely satisfying. The parable was looking as though it was going to be a thoroughly edifying tale with a moral along the lines of 'those who despise their family obligations ultimately find themselves without friends in time of need'. Or, to add a little to a biblical verse, 'The wages of sin are not just death but a shameful and painful death among pigs.' There may, of course, have been those who had the uneasy feeling that Jesus was going to put a little twist in somewhere. They were right.

Before going on, let's stand back from the facts and consider some of the issues raised. Let's consider the father in this parable. Although he is more central in the second act, there are issues here. The first centres on the fact that we live in an age where, sadly, many people have a real problem with father figures. Some have known actual abuse from their fathers; some are just aware that their fathers have not been figures they look up to with respect. So, faced with a parable that centres around a father they know is going to turn out to be – in some way – a model of God, they find themselves tensing up. 'I cannot see God as Father,' they protest. Let's say at the outset that we understand this. But what can be done about it? Although there is a lot to be said for talking in general of God as 'our parent' rather than a father, any radical solution involving the removal from the Bible of all language about God as Father is unworkable. To do that would be to dismantle not just this parable, but a lot of other things too. Although it may sound trite, the situation is not dissimilar from that of someone who has been cheated by being given fake money. You cannot give up using money; you just have to draw a distinction between the bogus and the genuine. Our suggestion is that you make a similar definite and repeated effort to distinguish between God as Father on the one hand, and your own troubled experience of a father figure on the other. So when you talk or think of God as Father, you may prefer to use the expression 'God the perfect caring Father'. If the very word *father* is problematic for you, then you may wish to use the Aramaic word *Abba* that Jesus used.

A second issue here is more theological. It is easy for a Christian to apply the doctrine of the Trinity to this parable and make the assumption that what we are talking about is specifically God the Father and *not* Jesus or the Holy Spirit. This, however, is to import a division that is not actually there in the text. (The doctrine of the Trinity – the Christian belief that God exists as three persons in one perfect unity – is there in the New Testament, but we must be wary of reading it into texts where it is not present.) It is far wiser and, as we will see, more profitable to consider the father as simply representing God.

The third issue is based around a question. Was the father right to let the son go? Should he have given his son the share of the estate, or should he simply have said 'no'? After all, most fathers would guess what was likely to happen and just say, 'Son, no way!' or, 'You must be joking!' The whole issue is complicated for Christians because if we take the father to be God, we may feel obliged to defend every aspect of the father's behaviour. After all, we say, if he is a picture of God, then he must be infallible and perfect. Yet here we may be going too far. It is worth noting that, in a way that we may find disconcerting, Jesus was perfectly happy using flawed people as images of God. So, for instance, in what is called the Parable of the Unjust Judge, Jesus talks about a harassed widow and a corrupt and lazy legal figure as parallels to the praying believer and God.[3] In another parable, he seems to commend a crooked steward.[4] In fact, sometimes characters in parables are closer to caricatures or even cartoon figures than real people. The reality is that, because parables are rarely allegories (and certainly not consistently worked-out allegories where *everything* represents something), we have to be careful in attributing meaning to details. In short, the Parable of the Prodigal is not at all concerned with whether or not the father was wise in this area. So, in answer to that almost universal parental problem, 'Should I allow my son or daughter to do what they want?' we have to admit that this parable probably says nothing of *specific* relevance. It is more concerned with how people are rescued from the fate of self-destruction than whether we should allow them to run the risk of that fate. The Parable of the Prodigal is not directly concerned with our issues over free will, but instead focuses on the son's restitution and the resulting responses. Yet having said this, there is no doubt that the way in which the son is allowed to rebel by the father can be seen as an illustration of the universal principle that, if you are going to treat people as responsible individuals, you must grant them the right to make a mess of things.

We must remember that parables may raise lots of questions, but they do not always answer them. As stripped down as the costume of an Olympic athlete, parables carry no unnecessary baggage. That rule helps us with another question: where is the mother in this parable? Well, if the drama was simply about spurned family love, then we might indeed expect reference to the mother. But it isn't: it's about the Prodigal's rejection of rights and duties and in this culture such matters were essentially a man's business. Before you accuse Luke of being complicit in cultural bigotry, remember that in the preceding parable, the central figure is a woman. To ask, 'Where is the mother in the Parable of the Prodigal?' is about as sensible as asking why Goldilocks wasn't at school!

Having put aside what the parable *doesn't* teach, let's consider what it *does* teach. The first point is this: many of us may find it easy to judge the Prodigal, but we may be less than fair to him. It is all too easy to criticise a man who has turned his back so drastically and hurtfully on both his family and his heritage. Yet for every individual who actually walks out of such a situation and travels those miles away, there are no doubt a hundred who wish they could bring themselves to do the same. It is probably completely realistic to imagine that the entire village watched as the son began his long journey away from all that he had come from. It is probably no less realistic to see in the silent and solemn crowd many who wished they had the guts to do likewise. What stopped them? In most cases probably simply a lack of courage. Before we judge the younger son, let us be honest with ourselves. If we haven't done what he did, is it because we had more principles or simply less courage? Sometimes the motivation for what seems to be a moral life is not so much the love of righteousness as the fear of consequences. It is all too easy for the outsider to confuse cowardice with morality. Famously, Jesus taught that we should judge motivations as much as actions. Sin, Jesus taught in the Sermon on the Mount, could be in the heart.[5] Perhaps we need to be honest and say that there is more of the Prodigal in us than we would like to admit.

6

The Prodigal: Act Two – The Restoration of the Younger Son

Let's start with the text.

> When he came to his senses, he said, 'How many of my father's hired servants have food to spare, and here I am starving to death! I will set out and go back to my father and say to him: Father, I have sinned against heaven and against you. I am no longer worthy to be called your son; make me like one of your hired servants.' So he got up and went to his father.
>
> But while he was still a long way off, his father saw him and was filled with compassion for him; he ran to his son, threw his arms around him and kissed him.
>
> The son said to him, 'Father, I have sinned against heaven and against you. I am no longer worthy to be called your son.'
>
> But the father said to his servants, 'Quick! Bring the best robe and put it on him. Put a ring on his finger and sandals on his feet. Bring the fattened calf and kill it. Let's have a feast and celebrate. For this son of mine was dead and is alive again; he was lost and is found.' So they began to celebrate.
>
> (Luke 15:17–24)

At the darkest hour, light dawns. Amid the misery and the pangs of hunger, the Prodigal comes to his senses. A plan emerges. He will return to his father and ask for employment. There is no hint of any expectation except that he might get an opportunity to work and thus be able to survive. So he rehearses his speech with its confession of guilt, its admission that he has forfeited the right to be a son and his eager desire to earn a living. With his hopes resting on charity, he turns homeward. In that brief but poignant verse we read, 'So he got up and went to his father.'

Let's pause here to note a couple of issues. Some commentators see in the son's action no more than a cold and calculated response to his pressing problems. On this view he comes up with a cunning and self-centred plan to enable him to get food for his stomach: 'How many of my father's hired servants have food to spare, and here I am starving to death!' This is not therefore true repentance and the planned speech is simply a way to try to regain a working relationship with his parent. (How many of us have devised similar speeches to try to get back in with our parents?) This interpretation is possible, yet the text surely indicates something of a genuine repentance. It is worth noticing that both here and later (v. 21) the Prodigal says, 'I have sinned against heaven and against you. I am no longer worthy to be called your son.' As we have already noted, in something as lean as a parable, any repetition is of vital importance. We must be in no doubt that the attitude of the son on returning to his village is very different from his attitude on leaving it. No doubt it was not perfect repentance, but then what repentance ever is?

Another significant feature is the recognition on the part of the younger son that his offence is not simply against his father, but against God. In the son's 'prepared statement' he says that he has not just sinned against his father, but also against heaven – in other words, God.* This is a sentiment expressed elsewhere in the Bible, notably by David in Psalm 51:4 and 2 Samuel 12:13. The sobering logic behind this is probably that, because all human beings are made in God's image and are – in a very real sense – owned by God, a sin against another human is ultimately a sin against God.

Finally, let's note a very practical point. There is something striking about the fact that the son acts on common sense. As has been widely commented, the great problem with common sense is that it is not common. Yet here he has realised that he must either return or perish. It may not seem the most awesome example of wisdom, but history is full of those who have chosen to starve rather than eat humble pie. How often have we heard someone say over some common-sense, logical solution, 'I'll be damned if I do that'? Reckless and rebellious he may have been, but the Prodigal knew when to turn home. Sometimes the best wisdom lies in nothing more dramatic than soberly evaluating all the facts of a case, coming to the right conclusions about them and acting on them.

To return to the parable, it is quite possible that even here, with the Prodigal Son returning homeward, the first hearers of this story would still have been expecting morality to triumph in the end. He had done wrong, he had been stupid and, to make it all worse, he had bankrupted himself. After committing such an appalling sin against his family, community and faith, the audience would have known that there was no option but for the son to be finally and completely rejected. Yet both they – and the Prodigal – are to be surprised by grace.

When we come to what is the high point of the parable, we find it almost impossible to condense Jesus' own words. 'But

* Pious Jews often use the word 'heaven' instead of 'God' for fear of breaking the second Commandment.

while he was still a long way off, his father saw him and was filled with compassion for him; he ran to his son, threw his arms around him and kissed him.' Was the father watching and waiting for the son? Did he, like the father in the story of the Salvadoris, regularly visit some watchtower that overlooked the winding road? We do not know. What we do know is that the sight of his son produced an overwhelming compassion. The father ran to his son.

We need to consider that little expression 'he ran'. In a culture based around honour and shame, no one other than children and athletes runs. To be slow, stately and dignified is to be honourable. To run is to become dishevelled, hot, sweaty and out of breath; it is to lose all dignity, and it is to gain shame.

Chris notes that in eight years of working at the American University of Beirut, he only once saw a senior member of the administration run and that was under such memorable conditions that it merits retelling. It was at the point when the Lebanese Civil War had come so uncomfortably close to the campus of the American University that shells were falling barely a kilometre away. Having been to the hospital to give blood – Chris figured it was the sort of day when they were going to use all they had – he carefully made his way back onto campus. At the gates he encountered not just an uneasy gaggle of university guards, but the head of security himself, a former army captain. The captain was a small man in late middle age whose smart uniform was strained by a rather substantial stomach. Normally amiable, he was now very nervous. After a rather hasty interchange of the appropriate formal greetings, he recommended that Chris really ought to take cover and suggested that they both go to the relative security of the guardhouse.

Together they began walking at a suitably dignified pace through the unnervingly empty university grounds. Suddenly there was the appalling whine of an incoming shell, the crump of an explosion, and the ground shook. As the wave of sound ebbed away, Chris could hear from somewhere beyond the university walls the faint metallic tinkle as shell fragments struck the ground. The captain gave him a worried glance and without a word the two of them very slightly increased their pace. Chris considered running for it, but felt it would be cowardly (the British also have their own standards of honour and shame).

Boom! There was a second deafening blast and this time the noise of the explosion and the chiming sounds of shrapnel were even louder. Now Chris saw the captain turn and look to see if his men were watching him. He suddenly realised that the captain was afraid of losing honour by running.

Boom! A third shell landed, this time so close that, as the shock-waves of the blast died away, Chris could hear the hot metal shards bouncing and clattering around on the road just outside the college wall.

The captain swallowed, seemed to hesitate, and then spoke. 'I think . . . Doctor Chris, that . . . we *run!*'

The fear of death meant that honour and dignity had to be sacrificed. The captain began to run stiffly towards the guardhouse – and Chris is not in the least ashamed to say that not only did he imitate the captain, but he got to safety well before him.

So in the parable, the father ran, and in so doing he shamed himself. Of course, the father was not alone; such men rarely are. They are always accompanied by aides, stewards and servants and, in troubled times, bodyguards. Certainly someone was there for the father to give orders to. The encounter between the father and the son was a public meeting and therefore what happened had public implications. We may safely presume that the way the father reacted, both in running and in showing grace and mercy to the son, was not universally appreciated. After all, the weighty matters of shame and honour do not belong to individuals alone, but to an entire community. For the father – the chief landowner – to do what he did was to bring shame on the entire community that was linked with him. His dishonour was their dishonour.

Here in the parable the tiny details pile up. There is no uneasy stand-off with both men trying to avoid each other's eyes as the son stutters out his apology. Instead, the father just embraces the son and kisses him. Yes, it is utterly poignant, but there is more than emotion here; there is acceptance. Judgement has been put to one side; the penalty has been withdrawn.

Despite the actions of his father, the son begins his speech. (How many times on the long journey had he rehearsed it?) 'Father, I have sinned against heaven and against you. I am no longer worthy to be called your son.' His final clause, 'make me like one of your hired servants', is cut short before it can be uttered. He never gets that far. Then, in one of those wonderful reversals in which the Bible delights, the father snaps out orders to those accompanying him: the son is to be given the best robe, a ring and sandals, and his return is to be celebrated by the best meal that can be arranged.

The accumulation of the details here is meant to make sure that we do not miss the significance of what is going on. The robe was not just to cover the dirt and nakedness (any old robe would have done that), but also to declare publicly, possibly in the face of hostility, that the Prodigal was restored as the son. The imagery of 'being covered' is a rich one in the Bible and through using it the father is asserting (no doubt before a rapidly gathering crowd) his attitude to the son. He is saying, in effect, 'I am putting my protection over my son. He is my responsibility. He comes under my authority and if that worries you, then you will have to deal with me.' The ring may well have been a signet ring, in which case it conveyed family authority. What about the sandals? They were presumably a mark that this man was now no servant or slave, but a son. The final order, that of the killing of the choice calf, is also significant. Such an animal would certainly have been enough to feed a small village. (There was no freezer to save any of the scraps!) Theoretically, some sort of restitution could have been carried out privately – perhaps a meeting with the father behind closed doors with some face-saving compromise agreed. But no, there is to be nothing of this: it is all to be out in the open. While the precise cultural significance of these elements (the robe, the ring, the sandals) is not entirely clear to us, their general import is plain. The son is freely, utterly and publicly restored. There are no conditions, no limitations and no secrecy.

We must not skim over the celebration. Look again at the text. 'Bring the fattened calf and kill it. Let's have a feast and celebrate. For this son of mine was dead and is alive again; he was lost and is found. So they began to celebrate.' There is much that is in it. For one thing, there is the celebration itself, an unmistakable link to the two preceding parables: both the lost and found sheep and the lost and found coin foreshadow the lost and found son. For another, these verses highlight the emphasis on rejoicing in this story. It might seem to be a hard task to overlook the note of joyful celebration that exists in these verses. Nevertheless, there have been treatments of this parable which effectively seem to do just that. We remind ourselves of where we came in: the Pharisees' failure to rejoice over the lost.

What is happening here? We will return to this later, but we must not skate over what is going on. The father, in breach of all convention and collective morality, has totally and utterly restored the younger son. The son's reinstatement is proclaimed in words ('this son of mine was dead and is alive again; he was lost and is found'), in symbols (the ring, the robe and the sandals) and in public action (the feast for the community). His wrongdoings, his stupidity and his failure ('he could at least have returned a financial success!') are all dismissed. The past episode is blotted out. He is now back where he was before it all started.

Here we see mercy, in that the penalties that could have been applied to him are not used. Justice demanded that the father turn him away. Indeed, it would have been most appropriate for some chief steward to send the son packing; after all, was he not now effectively dead? The son was hoping for mercy – the mercy that would remove any penalty and allow him to get a job as a servant. But we see here more than mercy: we see grace. It is worth distinguishing between the two. Mercy removes punishment. If you like, it removes bad debts. It is essentially a negative process, the removal or neutralisation of something bad. Grace goes further and is a positive process; it doesn't simply remove the bad, it adds the good. Not only is the sentence of judgement lifted, but also the son is restored to a position of honour and responsibility. He sought mercy, but he found grace.

Are we to make anything of the son's silence? Those of us who are parents would love to read that the son said, 'Oh thanks, Dad! I've been so stupid!' and that he fell down at his father's feet with tears of gratitude streaming down his face. The parable says nothing of this. Indeed, from now on, the younger son walks off stage. Perhaps he did say 'thanks' and express his repentance. Perhaps he didn't. You see, grace is a risk because it can be refused or abused. If you offer grace with conditions, it isn't grace. God expects his children to offer grace to others, but he gives no guarantee that it will be an effective strategy.

It is no wonder that this parable is such a favourite with Christians, because it speaks very strongly of the extraordinary truth at the heart of the gospel. The good news (which is what the word *gospel* means) is not simply that those who are God's enemies are forgiven. However welcome that might be, such an action would simply be mercy. What we are offered is something beyond mercy: we are offered *grace*. God does not simply declare us innocent, but restores us (like the Prodigal) to be his honoured and beloved children.

So, as the saying goes, 'all's well that ends well'. We might have considered that the parable should end at this point. But it doesn't. It twisted once to send the Prodigal Son home. Now it twists again.

7

The Prodigal: Act Three – The Rebellion of the Elder Son

The last act of the parable reads as follows:

> Meanwhile, the older son was in the field. When he came near
> the house, he heard music and dancing. So he called one of
> the servants and asked him what was going on. 'Your brother
> has come,' he replied, 'and your father has killed the fattened
> calf because he has him back safe and sound.'
>
> The older brother became angry and refused to go in. So
> his father went out and pleaded with him. But he answered his
> father, 'Look! All these years I've been slaving for you and never
> disobeyed your orders. Yet you never gave me even a young
> goat so I could celebrate with my friends. But when this son
> of yours who has squandered your property with prostitutes
> comes home, you kill the fattened calf for him!'
>
> 'My son,' the father said, 'you are always with me, and every-
> thing I have is yours. But we had to celebrate and be glad,
> because this brother of yours was dead and is alive again; he
> was lost and is found.'
>
> (Luke 15:25–32)

This final act is so tightly told that we have to consider carefully what is going on. Nevertheless, knowing that the elder son, who dominates this act, is clearly meant to represent the Pharisees helps our interpretation.

We are told that the elder son was in the field, presumably working or, more likely, in charge of workers. Alerted by the sound of festivities, he calls one of the servants and enquires about the reason. Does he already guess at the cause? His anger rises. It is hard not to see a nod here to the first crime of the Bible, described in Genesis 4, where we read of two sons, Cain and Abel. Cain, the elder, becomes angry over the superiority of his younger brother's sacrifice to God, flies into a rage and kills him. Although there is no mention of violence in this parable, we need to be aware of the potential for it. Is Jesus hinting in this story that he knows the hostility of the Pharisees may go beyond angry words? We need to realise that the issues between Jesus and the Pharisees are not the harmless verbal wrestlings of armchair theologians. In both parable and reality, violence is on the horizon.

The elder son's fury manifests itself in a stubborn refusal to go in and join the festivities. By now you are probably sufficiently sensitive to the world of shame, honour and the extended family to realise that for him to do this is a grotesque and flagrant breach of social standards. In such a culture, the elder son's task (whether he likes it or not is irrelevant) is to be completely and utterly supportive of the father. As 'heir to the throne' it is his duty to stand alongside his father, lend him support and act as his right-hand man. This solidarity between the generations is a vital survival mechanism: for the family to continue to exist, there must be a perfect transition of power. So for the elder son to refuse to go in to the feast is for him to deliver the most public of slaps in the face of his father.

It is no doubt significant that the father goes to plead with his son. He could simply have sent a rebuke or just ignored him.

Instead he goes out personally to try to rebuild the relationship. Despite this effort, the response he receives is chilling: 'Look! All these years I've been slaving for you and never disobeyed your orders. Yet you never gave me even a young goat so I could celebrate with my friends. But when this son of yours who has squandered your property with prostitutes comes home, you kill the fattened calf for him!'

Most of us have been involved, to our regret, in shouting matches where the accusations fly around. '*You* never wrote', '*You* never phoned', '*You* forgot our anniversary', 'It was *your* idea to come here for a holiday.' We recognise such language here. Indeed, the elder son's words are so full of bitterness, anger and contempt that they almost form an encyclopaedia of verbal abuse. There is utter *disrespect*: notice the brusque way in which the son fails to use any expression such as 'My father' in his reply. There is *distortion*: the protest that he has 'been slaving' for his father is incorrect, as we have already been told that the property was divided, so the elder son now owns two-thirds of the estate. There is the *transfer of blame*: 'you never gave me even a young goat' – in other words, 'It's all *your* fault!' There is almost certainly *exaggeration*: was he really never given the opportunity to have a barbecue with his friends? There is a blatant *nastiness*: he says that his brother had not merely lived wildly, but had 'squandered your property with prostitutes'. Does he really know that? Isn't he simply trying to portray his brother in the worst possible light? There is *disassociation*: his refusal to name his brother, simply referring to him as 'this son of yours', is striking. There is *insinuation*: '*I* never brought shame on my family.' (Do we not feel the cold, self-righteous pride here?)

What lies behind all this? Here we must be cautious, because quite simply we are not told. (One reason for creating a story around the Prodigal, as we have, is that it allows you to separate imagination from legitimate interpretation.) Obviously, the trigger is the return and restoration of the younger son. Now it cannot be that the elder son is primarily troubled by the financial impli-cations of the return – as it were from the dead – of his prodigal brother; the estate has already been divided. No, what appals him is the fact that, far from being disciplined, the younger son has been welcomed back and restored to his position. All family honour, all decency has been utterly thrown away; the most basic codes of moral behaviour have been broken.

It is hard not to sympathise with the elder son's anger. Imagine you had worked in a factory for years as a loyal employee, slowly and patiently climbing your way up the ladder through solid hard work and painstaking reliability. Now imagine the existence of a colleague who had joined the firm with you, but who, years later, had suddenly and spectacularly left for a job with a competitor, taking along trade secrets and skills. And now imagine how you would feel if you went into work one Monday and found your former colleague not simply brought back into the firm, but appointed to the same level as you. 'It's not fair!' you would cry. Your fury would be considerable: after all, there is no anger quite as powerful as that fuelled by moral indignation. This is the basis of the elder son's fury and it is hard to deny that he has a case. Yet there may be more still. It is worth considering that when the father gave the returning Prodigal the robe, ring, sandals and fat-tened calf, he was handing out things that now belonged as much to the elder brother as to him; after all, hadn't the property been divided? We may be fairly sure that the elder brother would have taken the view that his father had exceeded his rights.

Yet it is impossible to read this story without sensing that there must be something more behind this open blast of verbal bitter-ness. The arrival of the younger son looks to be not so much the cause of the explosion, but the trigger for something that has been accumulating over many years. Without plumbing any depths of speculative psychoanalysis, what is surely revealed here is the fact that the elder son is already separated from his father. For all his fine language (*'I've* slaved for you and *I've* never disobeyed your orders'), what we see here is a son whose relationship with his father is disastrously inadequate. He may be a family member in body, but he has been absent in spirit; in that memorable phrase, 'the wheel is turning but the hamster's dead'. The sad fact now revealed is that the father had *two* rebellious sons. The younger one knew he was rebellious and acted on it; the elder might not have acted on his rebellion initially (did he ever acknowledge that he was rebelling?), but it all burst out in the end. We talked earlier about the possibility of being a 'prodigal of the heart': someone who wanted to rebel, but did not have the courage to do so. It is hardly beyond possibility that the elder son's cold dislike of the Prodigal was because his brother had done what he had never had the courage to do.

There may be other matters. It seems that in a Jewish family of the time, the elder son would have had some responsibility for reconciliation. Did he try to reconcile the younger son with his father when he demanded his inheritance and packed his bags? Or did he, with a cold shrug of his shoulders, stand back and let the rebellion occur? If he was supposed to be a reconciler, his anger now is even more blameworthy.

Incidentally, there are very close links here with another one of Jesus' tales, the Parable of the Two Sons. This reads as follows:

'What do you think? There was a man who had two sons. He went to the first and said, "Son, go and work today in the vineyard."

'"I will not," he answered, but later he changed his mind and went.

'Then the father went to the other son and said the same thing. He answered, "I will, sir," but he did not go.

'Which of the two did what his father wanted?'

'The first,' they answered.

> Jesus said to them, 'Truly I tell you, the tax collectors and
> the prostitutes are entering the kingdom of God ahead of you.
> For John came to you to show you the way of righteousness,
> and you did not believe him, but the tax collectors and the
> prostitutes did. And even after you saw this, you did not repent
> and believe him.'[1]

Here we have a first son who initially rebels, but who later comes round to doing his father's will, and a second son who is dutiful in word, but rebellious in action. Here, too, it is the first son who ultimately ends up as the truly obedient child.

The nature of the relationship exposed here is of enormous significance. The elder son's words, 'I've been slaving for you and never disobeyed your orders', are not those of a son, but of a servant. His vocabulary is drawn from the world of business and employment and he sees his relationship with his father as one that revolves around duties, commands and rewards. His allegations towards his father would not be out of place in some legal discussion in an industrial tribunal over 'breach of contract'. If we remember that the rebellious younger brother wanted to come back as a servant, we will see a deliberate irony in the way that this son sees himself as exactly that. The tone and the words suggest a cold, formal and distanced relationship between son and father.

The blatant bitterness of the elder son is heightened by the way that he tries to accuse his father in the words, 'You never gave me even a young goat.' There is an echo here of yet another parable, the one commonly called the Parable of the Talents, where three servants are given sums of money to manage during their master's absence.[2] The third servant does nothing with the money and when he is asked by the returning master to justify his behaviour, he says this: '"Master," he said, "I knew that you are a hard man, harvesting where you have not sown and gathering where you have not scattered seed. So I was afraid and went out and hid your gold in the ground. See, here is what belongs to you.'"[3] Here, as in the Parable of the Prodigal, the defence centres on a self-justification based around a denigration of the one in authority.

Let us move our focus from the parable to its context. Here, unmistakably, Jesus is pointing out to his critics that the only relationship we can have with God is one based on grace. As elsewhere in the Gospels, Jesus makes the point that actions and rituals are not enough to put us right with God.[4] No one, even the most saintly of us, can ever earn a right relationship with God. That is the bad news. The good news is that we can enter into such a relationship by accepting our heavenly Father's gracious gift of forgiveness. Indeed – and here is the real tragedy of the Pharisees past and present – to try to demand a relationship on the basis of what we have done is utterly counterproductive. It is to rule out the possibility of a family relationship. God doesn't do business relationships; he only does family ones. It is as if heaven is a splendid house with two doors. The front door is large, formal and imposing and the human race always tries to enter by it, hammering on it and loudly declaring their rights to enter. Yet that door remains closed. Meanwhile, the rear door – much less grand – is unlocked and opens easily to all who, with humble manner and repentant tone, ask for entrance.

The elder son shows no love whatsoever for his father and none for his brother. There are echoes here of Jesus' teaching that the greatest commandments are first, to love God and second, to love others.[5] In the elder brother's evident resentment towards his father we see a parallel to the lack of love towards God, our heavenly Father. In his sullen refusal to accept his brother's return, we see an equal lack of love towards others. In his words we hear not just the vocabulary of the business world; we hear someone who is hopelessly self-centred. His readiness to ruin his father's party has all the air of a selfish tantrum.

The final words of the parable belong to the father. "'My son,'" the father said, "you are always with me, and everything I have is yours. But we had to celebrate and be glad, because this brother of yours was dead and is alive again; he was lost and is found.'"

There is much we would like to fill in here and we need to exercise restraint in our interpretation. However, this is not a story that exists in isolation. For one thing, we know who Jesus is targeting, and for another, there are linkages to a vast weight of other teaching both from Jesus and from elsewhere in the New Testament.

The father points out that the elder son has misunderstood – or misrepresented – their relationship. In truth, there has been nothing held back. All that he owns has been available for the son to use. The implication here is that, had the son wanted to have a goat for his friends, then he should have asked for one. This failure of the son to ask is a pointer to the heart of the problem. Why didn't he make any such request? Surely it was because he saw himself as being independent of his parent: he had no need of the father. Sometimes independence from a parent can be a virtue: 'I'm standing on my own two feet now,' says a child happily as he or she gets a first pay cheque. Yet sometimes the desire for independence is wrong. It celebrates not self-sufficiency or a coming-of-age, but alienation or rejection. To boast that we don't ask God for anything may only be a hair's breadth away from proclaiming our rebellion. Whether we like it or not, we are designed to be dependent on God. In many places in the Gospels we find the teaching that God is delighted when we ask things of him.[6] Declaring our independence from God is perilously close to proclaiming that we do not need him. No relationship can exist on that basis.

This chapter began with Jesus talking of the necessity of celebration and gladness when those who were lost were found. The Parable of the Prodigal returns to this theme in its closing words. The one who was dead is now alive; the one who was lost is now found. Rejoicing is the only fitting response.

And here the parable ends. You might wonder – as some have – whether something is missing. Was there perhaps, you think, another paragraph that somehow Luke or the early copyists carelessly omitted? If you have placed too much emphasis on the younger son, then it is perhaps natural to see it this way. If this story was simply about God's loving heart to the lost, then the ending *is* oddly abrupt. Yet if, following the preceding two parables and the context, you see the parable as being fundamentally addressed to the 'religious', concerning their surly and bitter attitude to those repentant sinners with whom Jesus was eating, then the ending makes utter sense. Of course, if it was a nursery tale, then it would be more neatly rounded: ' . . .and they all lived happily ever after.' But parables and nursery tales are actually very different. The open-ended nature of this story is typical of a parable. The very way it is left hanging invites us to speculate and invokes our own involvement. It is as if Jesus is saying to his opponents, 'You stand there with the Father just as the elder brother did. You also are faced with two choices. The first is that you say (however reluctantly), "Very well, Father. I agree with you. My brother's return is so wonderful that I must celebrate." And then, together with your father, you go back into the festivities. The second is that you shake your fist against him, tell him again what you think of him and . . .'

And *what*? In the account of Cain and Abel, anger led to murder. Jesus may very well be hinting that the elder son's dislike and resentment of the father may build up to a point at which he lashes out physically. After all, as the elder son might have argued, what is right has to be protected. The family, society, even the faith have to be preserved. You can't just go around freely forgiving people. Forgiveness must be rationed and doled out only to the deserving.

Of course, the open-ended nature of the Parable of the Prodigal speaks not just to the Pharisees of Jesus' generation. The two possible outcomes are the two roads that lie open before all men and women. One road – that of reconciliation – can be taken by agreeing with God's grace and celebrating over those who are won through it. The second road – rejection – is to disagree with God's gift of grace and to seek to work against it and the God who is central to it. To take that second highway of rejecting God's grace is a serious and momentous decision. For when you gaze along that road, you can see something of where it ends: at a tall, stark cross and a mob bawling, 'Crucify!'

8

Conclusions

This parable is, in fact, all about a single enormous subject, grace, and how we respond to it. However, before we look at that, we need to address what we might call 'the elephant in the room'. For those unfamiliar with the term, 'the elephant in the room' is the object that is so big and so obvious that no one talks about it because everybody takes its presence for granted. Here in this parable, curiously ignored by many, we have a remarkable elephant in the room. This particular elephant is the parable's author.

The astonishing nature of this story – its celebration of outrageous, convention-breaking grace, its reckless dismissal of social standards, its criticism of those whose religion is duty and whose duty is religion – requires an equally astonishing author. It is a story that proclaims the need for radical forgiveness, gracious restoration and the unreserved celebration of those who have betrayed our best interests and undermined all we stand for. In doing so, it subverts the framework of all organisations and sabotages all authority structures. Some people are surprised that the Parable of the Prodigal is only preserved in one Gospel. To be honest, the real wonder is that it was preserved by any. Is it too fanciful to imagine some early church leader looking up from the scroll that has just been presented to him, frowning, scratching his beard in thought and then saying, 'My dear Luke, are you *absolutely* sure the Lord said this? If there is any doubt, I really think we ought to omit it. It . . . could be misinterpreted'? Quite simply, there can only be one reason why this parable was preserved by the early church: it was taught by a man whose authority was so great that it could not be disputed and whose every word – however unpalatable – was to be treasured.

There is an almost constant pressure to whittle down the cosmic figure of Jesus that the Church has traditionally presented to that of a roving peasant preacher within Judaism who taught little more than religious clichés and whose miraculous powers and outrageous claims are merely the result of the imaginative spin doctors of the early church. We may honour him with the word 'prophet', but we do not treat him as Lord. Of course, to reduce Jesus to an unremarkable figure ignores the difficulties of how you derive an early church marked by joyful dynamism, unyielding certainty and overflowing enthusiasm from such a bland, colourless and utterly anonymous character. Prophets, revolutionaries and storytellers were (and are) two-a-penny in the Middle East, but only one has ever been worshipped by his contemporaries as God made flesh. The existence of a parable like this – and indeed the whole dynamic social explosion of the early church – only makes sense if behind it was a truly extraordinary person with truly extraordinary authority. The claims of Christians from the earliest days to the present are that Jesus of Nazareth was a figure with just such an authority. Behind the Prodigal (and the Church) lies the towering authority of Jesus. The early church saw this authority as having a threefold basis: Jesus had an authority that he claimed by his words, an authority that he demonstrated by his miracles, and an authority that was authenticated by his resurrection. That authority was so overwhelming that what he said was, quite literally, gospel truth. He was, in every respect, Lord.

To treat the Parable of the Prodigal seriously necessitates that we treat its author seriously too. There is much more we could say here, but we must make the point that Christianity has always taught that the author of this story is not, like all other authors of the distant or recent past, dead and buried. He still lives and can be known. The ultimate issue here is not whether we decide to praise or criticise Jesus as some long-dead teller of tales, but whether we come to know him as living Lord and personal friend. It cannot be too strongly stated that whatever else our conclusions, if we miss Jesus in this parable, we miss everything. With all other writings of the past, the question posed is, 'What do I make of this author?' With the Parable of the Prodigal, our concern should be, 'What does this author make of me?'

THE THEME

At the start of this chapter we said that the parable is fundamentally about a single subject: grace. Let us now turn to that great overarching theme. The background helps us. Quite frequently, the careful Bible reader finds that the chapter divisions are a hindrance, not a help, and a question often arises as to why they were inserted where they were. Yet here in Luke the divisions make sense: all three parables in chapter 15 belong together. Each one of the three is to do with something that is lost and each deals with the right response to its recovery. Taken together, they form a progression. In the first parable, what is lost is a sheep and it has to be sought in a way that involves effort and cost. In the second parable, what is lost is something even more valuable, a coin, and that too must be sought with effort and cost. In both cases, there is rejoicing when the lost object is found. In the third parable, what is lost is a son. Significantly, he is not sought; he must return on his own. Nevertheless, a long way from home he is met by his father and forgiven and restored in a way that involves his parent in pain and cost. Here, too, when the lost is found there is rejoicing.

Yet it is at the very end of this parable that Jesus sets up a deliberately jarring note, one that would have had his enemies sitting up in discomfort. The rejoicing is not universal. His brother rejects the son's restoration. This is a classic argument of comparisons. In effect, Jesus first asks this question: 'Do you agree that celebration is appropriate with a recovered sheep?' The answer is presumably, 'Yes.' He then poses – in effect – a supplementary question: 'Do you agree that celebration is appropriate when a valuable coin is recovered?' Again we may presume the answer is, 'Yes.' The final parable then delivers the knockout blow: 'Mustn't you also agree that celebration is appropriate when something infinitely more valuable – a human being – is recovered?'

This chapter is about being lost and being found; it is about being restored back to God. It is, in a real sense, about returning home. In a single sweet word, it is about *grace*. Grace is an awesome and enthralling word that defines one of the hallmarks of genuine Christianity. Many people outside the faith would acknowledge that grace is at the centre of the Christian faith. And yet what does grace really mean? We have already said that it is more than mercy, but we need to go further. One of the more interesting films of 2006 was *Amazing Grace*, an account of William Wilberforce's long and heroic fight against slavery. There was much that was good about that film, but one thing that many people found frustrating was that nowhere did it explain either what grace was or exactly *why* it was 'amazing'. A fascinating feature of the story of the Prodigal is the way that it reveals exactly what grace is all about.

Let's suggest that we see five grace-focused points in the parable. The first two lay something of an essential foundation for considering the subject; the last three address how we are to live in the light of grace.

1. GRACE DEFINED

Let's suggest a definition of grace here: *grace is unconditional kindness given to an undeserving recipient at an uncomfortable cost*. In this definition, grace has three elements and the Parable of the Prodigal shows all of them.

First, there is *unconditional kindness*. It is important that we realise that grace is unconditional: there are no terms to be met. If there were, it would not be grace; it would be either something that was earned, or a negotiated surrender. There is in grace an astonishing freeness; it is something that is truly given. Here in the parable we see the very model of unconditional grace. The father receives back his son with the simplest but most deeply felt act of acceptance. There is no setting out of terms of restitution, no demands for an apology, no stipulations about repayment, no rulings for better behaviour in the future. It is a free acceptance.

This highlights one of the interesting and alarming elements of grace: it is astonishingly risky. Unlike the story with which we began this book, we do not know the ending of the Parable of the Prodigal. Of course, there is a very high probability that the younger son (no doubt a sadder and wiser man) will, from now on, be a faithful and grateful son to his father. Yet it is only a probability; there is no guarantee. To offer grace is to take dangerous risks. It is to start a story without knowing its ending.

The grace shown to the younger son is, of course, a miniature picture of the grace that God shows to us human beings. He declares himself ready freely to wipe the slate clean, proclaims unilateral peace with his bitterest opponents and holds out to us the prospect of a new and restored relationship with himself. And he does so unconditionally. Like all of us, you have no doubt had your interest aroused by some apparently magnanimous advertisement ('Free holiday!' or, 'Money back!' or, '50 per cent discount!'), only to lose interest when, in the clauses at the end, you see the restrictions. Our heavenly Father makes no such deceptive promises; grace is kindness unfettered by conditions. God does not do small print.

Now to say this is not to say that there are no implications linked with grace. Think back to the parable. The son has been restored back to the family. But as we all know – or ought to know – being part of a family is a two-way matter. There are indeed rights and privileges, but there are also responsibilities and commitments. So it is with the Christian life. We enter under unconditional grace; our status is changed from rebels and enemies to sons and daughters of God. We are, to use a word that the New Testament uses, *adopted*. The concept of adoption has changed little in two thousand years and we can easily identify with it. We would all agree that to be adopted into a family is far more than simply having your name changed on some identity document. To be truly an adopted son or daughter is to engage fully in all that the family stands for, to come to relate closely to other family members, to share in the family values and to work together with others for its success. The same principle applies in the spiritual realm; if we really are Christians, we will show by changed lives, values and relationships that our adoption has been more than just a name change. Yes, grace is without conditions, but it is not without obligations.

If the first feature of grace is unconditional kindness, the second feature is that it is offered to an *undeserving recipient*. Consider the parable. The younger son had brought shame on the family and had dragged their honour into the gutter. All he deserved was judgement, but instead he received restoration. This models the way that grace is shown to us. Every single human being has sinned and rebelled against God. We have all despised his values and rejected his rule. We have all been like the Prodigal. Some of us have been spectacularly so, and have indeed spent time in that 'distant country'. Some of us have been less spectacular rebels and we may have lived lives apparently conforming to God's standards, yet in our hearts we know that we have been prodigals. We all deserve nothing. Indeed, the New Testament letters go much further. In the letter to the Romans, the apostle Paul says that we deserve God's judgement.[1] Even Christians can often find this hard to believe. We can come to imagine that God saw something in us that was worthwhile and deserving of his kindness. Yet the Bible is clear that we all deserve nothing and it is only by grace that we are restored back to God's family. If we *did* deserve anything, grace would not be grace; it would not be a gift, but a wage. A grace-less Christianity would not be fundamentally different from any other religion. The awesome and explosive nature of the good news of the Christian gospel is that God's kindness is offered without conditions to those who are utterly undeserving.

The third feature of grace joins unconditional kindness and an undeserving recipient: an *uncomfortable cost*. For grace to be truly grace, there must be a price. The whole point about grace is that, although there is no cost to the one who receives grace, there is a cost to whoever gives it. No one really knows who first coined the expression 'no such thing as a free lunch', but it expresses a fundamental reality of the universe. So in chemistry, matter cannot be created or destroyed: what is lost in one reaction must be gained in another. In physics we see the same: energy may change state, but can never be lost or gained. The same rigid laws of transfer and exchange apply with grace. If grace is given to someone, the giver must pay. To offer someone forgiveness without it costing you anything is great, but it is not grace. Grace costs.

We see this principle set out stark and clear in the Parable of the Prodigal. The younger son is indeed forgiven at the end of the story, but who has paid for that forgiveness? The answer, often overlooked by Western readers of the parable, is that the father pays by taking on public shame and dishonour. What goes on is an awesome symmetrical transfer. The father takes away the son's shame by losing his own honour; he restores the son's honour by suffering shame himself. In short, he pays the price.

What Jesus hints at here, the rest of the New Testament develops. The letters of Paul and the others speak much of grace and they often use the language of transfer and exchange. So we read that

Christ on the cross became cursed so that the curse of sin might be lifted from us.[2] We find out that Jesus was sacrificed so that we might receive righteousness.[3] We are told that he bore God's anger so that we might know God's forgiveness.[4] He was wounded so that we might be made whole.[5] Like the father in the parable, God (Father, Son and Spirit) paid the price for us prodigals to be brought back home. In the shameful abomination of the cross we see a cosmically scaled-up version of the father wrapping his cloak around the wretchedness of the son.

Here a brief aside is important. It is sometimes argued that there is an unbridgeable gap in the New Testament between the teaching of Jesus and the teaching of Paul. It is argued that Paul's declaration that we are made right by faith in Christ apart from any human effort is very different from what Jesus taught. Yet it is clear here that the good news of Paul and the good news of Jesus are the same: they centre on the fact that God in his sacrificial grace willingly and freely grants forgiveness and a new relationship to those who come to him in repentance and faith.

All three elements of grace – unconditional kindness, an undeserving recipient and an uncomfortable cost – meet in the Parable of the Prodigal.

2. THE GOD OF GRACE

There is always the very greatest danger that we make God in our own image. We read in Genesis 1 that he made us in his image; the temptation has always been that we return the favour by remaking him in ours. One of the most common ways of doing this is to ascribe to God those features that we either possess ourselves or admire in others. So the painter says, 'I like to see God as a great artist.' The numerically gifted person says, 'I like to think of God as the ultimate mathematician.' This process can also be much more subtle and more dangerous. Those people with a psychology dominated by rigid rules can easily come to think of God as solemn and severe, while those who are free and easy-going see God as the very opposite. To reshape God as we want him to be is very attractive, but it is not very wise. It is vital that our image of God is determined not by what we would like him to be, but by what he himself says that he is.

We need to remind ourselves that this parable – and the many other teachings of the Bible with which this story interlocks – is not how humans think of God, but how he defines himself. It is therefore the most helpful corrective we can have to wrong thinking about God. It is because of the importance of this parable that we spent some time looking at its authorship. After all, *authorship* and *authority* have more in common than their first six letters. If this parable goes back to Jesus, then, as he claimed to be uniquely qualified to tell us the truth about God, it has astonishing significance.

It is also important to think about the person of God in this context because there is also the danger that we think of grace as some cold, abstract process. Indeed, thinking about it as we just have done in terms of 'transfer' and 'exchange' can make it all seem a mechanical matter, the working out of some impersonal law of the universe. The fact is that grace is how God deals with each of us as a person. He loves us, and grace describes how that love works in practice. The New Testament does not invite us to take part in a chemical reaction ('Have your sins washed whiter than white!'), but to have our relationship with God healed and to join his family. If grace is the process at the heart of the parable, then God is the person at its heart.

The sidelining of God as a person has a long and troubled history in Christianity. One of the problems the early church faced when it spread beyond Palestine was that it began to interact with and absorb some of the views of Greek philosophy about God. The Greek philosophers, for the most part, saw God as a being who was so unchanging (the technical word is *immutable*) that he could not have emotions. That view became influential within Christianity, so that the biblical concept of God as a person who loves, cares and grieves over people became marginalised. The trend has continued and it is very common today to meet people who talk about God in terms of a designer or cosmic architect. Indeed, the God they describe often has more in common with the 'Force' of *Star Wars* than with the loving, living personal God of the Bible. In reality, the worship of such a remote figure is remarkably unsatisfactory. This sort of God may help us have an answer to such abstract philosophical questions as why the universe exists, but we can no more have a relationship with him than we can with gravity. Such a belief is dangerous to faith: its end product is a sterile religion that has little in common with the living and vibrant Christianity of the New Testament.

Those of us who might be tempted to believe in this kind of distant, cold and passionless God need to think carefully about this parable and, in particular, about the image of the father. We need to gaze at him running down the road, cloak flying, arms thrown wide, a picture of loving welcome at the sight of his long-lost son. This is our God. This image embodies the well-known verse in John's Gospel, 'For God so *loved* the world that he gave his one and only Son, that whoever believes in him shall not perish but have eternal life.'[6] Grace exists because God is a God of love. Grace is the principle on which he operates: it reflects God's heart.

We cannot explore here all the issues that this raises – of how justice and love can be matched, of reconciling the reality of pain, suffering and loss with a God of grace, of avoiding the dangers of placing God's love against his justice. All we can do here is to remind you that our relationship with God must always be rooted in the basis that he is a God of love who operates through grace. No other relationship is possible. We must live by grace and we must die by grace.

3. THE NEED TO RECEIVE GRACE

We have laid the foundations; let us now look at the implications for how we live in the light of God's grace. There are three implications and they follow the three characters – and therefore the three acts – of the parable.

Let us turn first to consider the younger son. He surely represents the entire human race, including all of us. We have all rebelled, all turned our back on our ancient inheritance, all rejected our loving God. There is something universal about the son's reckless departure from the family home. On the one hand, it looks backwards into the misty past and repeats that mysterious rebellion at the dawn of the human race when our ancestors walked out of Eden. On the other hand, it looks forward down the ages to our own personal and private rebellion against God. The Christian verdict is simply put: if we have not yielded our life to Christ, we are there in that distant land lost among pigs and self-despair and exiled from the Father. We need to return home.

For those who recognise themselves in this description, this parable offers much encouragement. Much of the work for the restoration of your relationship has been done. God has set his love upon you and is preparing to greet you; he will not just meet you halfway, but will run to meet you. What you could not do, he has done: the process of restitution is all but complete. It only remains for you to do two things. The first involves you making a decision to return to God. To use the language of the parable, you need to rise up from where you are in that distant land and return homeward. You alone know what that will mean for you in reality. What we can promise is that if you turn to God in sincerity, you will find him more than ready to meet you.

Second, we must receive God's gracious offer of restoration. Here our first thought may be that this seems strange. Why would anybody refuse the Father's grace? Yet if we consider the parable again, we are struck with the possibility that the younger son could have refused to receive the offer of a restored relationship with his father. After all, he had planned to ask to be treated as a servant. He could have rejected his father's offer, protesting that being a servant was quite good enough for him. The fact is that there are such people and we have met them. When offered God's rich grace, they spurn it. 'I don't think that would be right,' you hear them say. 'I prefer to try to earn my way with God.'

The fact is that, while grace is wonderful, it can be difficult to receive. To accept God's free pardon means that we must reject any possibility of earning our way with God. We must humbly bow our heads before him and accept his verdict. To accept grace is to admit defeat. The tragic irony is that it is precisely the moral people, the good people and those who count themselves as successful keepers of rules and regulations, who find grace hard. It is those like the younger son in the parable and the tax collectors and sinners around Jesus who find grace easy to accept. After all, they have no other card to play. They are in no position to be tempted to try to negotiate an alternative. For them, grace is the only show in town.

The reality is that we have all – to a greater or lesser extent – rebelled against God. There are only two classes of human being: those who are prodigals, and those who were prodigals. For those who are prodigals, the only difference is how distant the country is to which they have fled. Some of us may be willing to admit that, for all our hopes, we have been reduced to the pathetic state of pig-minding. Some of us have yet to recognise that unhappy truth.

We all need to enter that relationship with God of being sons and daughters greeted by a loving father. Yet what does this parable say to those who have already been in such a relationship for some time? Is this only a parable for those entering the Christian life? On the contrary, this parable speaks to us great words of comfort and blessing. We do not simply enter the Christian faith by grace, we continue it by grace. In particular, there is a tremendous blessing for all who are beset by problems and fears about their status with God. Remember how the father ran to the son, had him clothed with his own best robe and gave him his ring of authority? So God in heaven deals with those who return to him as prodigals. He clothes them with his protection and authority. He declares in the presence of all who accuse them – in both the earthly and spiritual realms – that they are indeed his precious sons and daughters.

We need to receive God's grace in order to enter the Christian life. Yet we are never able to stray from that principle of grace; it remains the rule for Christian living from beginning to end.

4. THE NEED TO REFLECT GRACE

Now let us turn to the father, that picture of God. We remind you that it is best to consider the father here as a picture of God in his awesome trinity, Father, Son and Spirit. All are involved in grace. Here we see the principle that we need to reflect grace. We use the word *reflect* with some care. The concept throughout the Bible is that those who come to know God then show his grace to others.

One danger is that people sometimes think that they should show grace to others in order that God will show grace to them. That is to distort things badly. Paradoxically, if we could earn grace, not only would it not be grace, but also we wouldn't need it. No, the priority is to come to God through grace first and then, aided by the power of God's Spirit, to show grace to others. As children imitate their parents, so we are to imitate our heavenly parent. We are to reflect God's grace to those around us.

This principle of 'reflecting grace' explains some passages in the New Testament that some people find problematic. So, for instance, in the Beatitudes of Matthew 5, we read, 'Blessed are the merciful, for they will be shown mercy.' A page or so further on we come to the Lord's Prayer, where we read, 'Forgive us our sins as we forgive those that sin against us.'[7] Those two statements can be interpreted as if they were referring to some sort of exchange deal – as if the believer could say, 'I will do this so that you will do that for me.' In fact, to think this is to turn everything on its head. These statements express not so much a deal, but rather a reciprocal obligation. It is much more along the lines of, 'I will do this because you have already done that for me.' Underlying both is the principle that those who know something of God's mercy and forgiveness should be those who show such qualities to others. Indeed, both verses make the same blunt point: if you are not able to show mercy and forgiveness, it may well indicate that you have not truly experienced it. The forgiven must forgive; those on whom mercy has been poured should pour out mercy on others. There is nothing in the entire universe as abnormal and inconsistent as the Christian who is unable to show grace to other people.

If we claim we are Christians – if we are those whose only plea before God is that we have found mercy through Christ – then we must show mercy to others. Whether it is at school, college, work or home, we need to be able to say, 'I forgive you: it's a forgotten matter,' and mean it. The issues surrounding forgiveness are so enormous that they could easily take another book; we will simply say here that we acknowledge that this is not an easy task. To forgive and restore, as the father in the parable no doubt knew (he certainly found out soon enough afterwards), is to expose your weakness, to invite attack and to lose honour. Forgiveness is far from easy; you may need all the help that God can give you to forgive. Thankfully, through God's Holy Spirit, we do have that help.

Yet in all the good that we do, we can take no real personal credit: we are merely reflecting God's grace. It is given to us in such abundance that it overflows from us into the lives of others.

5. THE NEED TO REJOICE IN GRACE

We have seen that, like the Prodigal, we need to receive grace and to reflect the grace of the Father. Now we must consider a final point of the parable: that we need to rejoice in grace. We remind ourselves that Jesus here was ultimately addressing the Pharisees. Now in one sense, the Pharisees are history. In another, they live on. Even those who enter the Christian life believing that they are wretched sinners and trusting only in God's grace to save them can, soon enough, begin to believe that they somehow deserved to be saved. What we see here is what we might call the Elder Brother Syndrome, a bitter and sullen refusal to rejoice in grace.

There are parallels here with the eternal triangle of romantic dramas. Here the triangle consists of the one shown grace, the one receiving grace and the unhappy third who is the bystander to grace. The elder brother here is the bystander and he doesn't like what he sees. Now, as we have noted earlier, it is unwise to dismiss his reaction too speedily. The brother has recognised what many of us might easily overlook: the fact that what the father has done is truly outrageous and shocking. There is an extraordinary and rather tragic irony here, in that the elder brother clearly understood all too well something of what grace was all about. He saw that grace was, to use our definition, 'unconditional kindness given to an undeserving recipient at an uncomfortable cost', and he rejected it utterly. This dislike of grace might have been because he loathed his younger brother. On the other hand – as was probably the case with many a Pharisee – it may have been not because he was immoral, but because, on the contrary, he *was* moral. The Pharisees and the elder brother saw that the principle of grace utterly undermined all the concepts of morality and ethics. They saw that if it was allowed to continue it would, at best, sideline religious rules and rituals and, at worst, destroy them altogether.

The problem of the Elder Brother Syndrome is that it did not die with the Pharisees. It is alive and well and curiously appealing. In fact, it is all too easy for Christians to adopt this position and it can manifest itself in at least two ways. The first way is that (perhaps having put a life of spectacular evil behind us) we gradually succumb to the temptation to think that God must feel rather pleased with us. This blinds us to the only basis on which we can ever live the Christian life: God's utterly undeserved grace to us in Jesus Christ. As we lose sight of grace, we begin to think that we can negotiate with God on something approaching equal terms. This is, of course, very untrue, unfortunate and unhealthy. Hand in hand with this is the fact that we soon begin to feel superior towards those who are outside the faith. We forget that we were once spiritual beggars ourselves and assume that our privileged status is something that we have earned. Having forgotten our own past, we therefore feel affronted when we sense God embracing some new convert and wrapping them in his best robe. This side of the grave, the temptation for us to become like the elder brother is always present. Indeed, the longer we are Christians, the greater the danger that we will forget that once upon a time we too were naked, dirty and wretched.[8] It is no bad thing to remind ourselves what we once were, or even what we might have been apart from the grace of God. 'There but for the grace of God go I' may be a cliché, but it is also a very real truth.

The second way of succumbing to Elder Brother Syndrome is related but more subtle. What happens to us as individuals is this: we enter the Christian faith through the happy realisation that we are saved by God's grace, but then, over the years, a degree of routine and even formality creeps into our relationship with God. So as private individuals we learn to manage and control some of our more difficult habits and we probably also acquire some good ones – prayer, Bible study, perhaps even some modest ability to forgive. More publicly, we become part of a church or a fellowship group, we become known as Christians and we may even take an open stand in the name of Christ against some public evil. Now all of these things – whether habits, values or actions – are good and are to be desired. Yet the peril lies here that increasingly we come to value these things not because they lead us to God, but because they are part of the routine of our lives. Slowly and surreptitiously, what were once the secondary features of our faith now take centre stage, and if we are not careful we will soon mistake them for that faith itself.

This is the problem with the elder brother and the Pharisees and their descendants. Ultimately they have come to major on the minors. The trappings have taken precedence over reality. Their faith has become like a marriage in which the couple are still going through all the formalities, but in which there is no love or passion. All is procedure, custom and routine: there is nothing at the core. Now if Christianity was a religion without grace and based entirely on rule-keeping, what they stood for would actually be sound practice. But for a religion founded on grace (and this includes both Old Testament Judaism and New Testament Christianity), this is a tragic mistake. They have indeed lost the plot: what was once relationship has now become religion; what was once lively rejoicing has now become dead ritual.

Let us give an illustration. Imagine that some man or woman creates a garden and plants in it a rich array of flowers and trees. Then, as it grows up, they build a wall around it in order to provide protection. Now imagine that, as the years pass, they come gradually to prize the wall more than the garden. We would consider this to be bizarre behaviour in the extreme. In the parable the elder brother is precisely like this. Matters that are secondary (family expectations) have taken the place of what should have been the highest priority (family relationships). This is a sad and all too common feature of the Christian life. Over time, secondary matters take priority over what should be our greatest good: knowing and loving God.

Rather than spend more time with the elder brother (who is fictional) and the Pharisees (who are extinct), we may be wiser to ask how we personally can maintain a right relationship with God in which we rejoice over his grace to others and to us. Fundamentally, we need to realise that our personal relationship with God lies at the heart of what we are. We have already seen that the relationship between father and elder son was strained, and there is a clue here. The relationship between God and us needs to be maintained. As it happens, the same rules apply for the relationship between God and us as with any other relationship. We need to stay close and we need to stay communicating. We need, too, to watch out for times when the rules and rituals become more important than the relationship. So we may start reading our Bibles and saying our prayers because we take pleasure from both, but there may come days when they become formal duties – things that we feel we have to do. That should be a warning sign that we need to make an effort to get back to God and recover something of the proper warmth that there should be in a relationship.

We need constantly to monitor our own faith to check that it is real. Remember that bitter comment from the elder brother that his father had never even given him a goat to share with his friends? We decided that this was probably simply a sour allegation. Nevertheless, it is probably not a bad idea to continue going to God to ask him for things for yourself and others. Of course, this might degenerate into pure selfishness, but a relationship tinged with selfishness is better than no relationship at all. It does at least encourage a spirit of dependence on God and brings us face to face with our need for grace.

It has to be said that not all forms of Elder Brother Syndrome are to do with individuals. There is a collective version, which is worth watching out for. It is interesting that in the Gospels, the Pharisees are almost always a group of people rather than an individual. They were concerned about the public and communal expression of their faith. In terms of their function, the Pharisees come close to those of us who are involved in church leadership. This should make us think. There is a particular problem in our churches that we tend to appoint professionals to do tasks, either those specifically trained in theological colleges or those who work in the week in skilled positions. Such people bring professional skills into the management of churches, which is generally a good thing: after all, chaos has no merits. Nevertheless, there is a danger that making the organisation run smoothly can somehow become far more important than anything else. A temptation exists for us to model our churches on business organisations and there can be few church leaders who have not sought, sometimes desperately, for polished and seamless services where everything happens at the right time in the right way. The danger is obvious: soon enough we start to create the church service either as an elaborate ritual or as a performance, and in doing so we begin to edge out that relationship with God that should be central.

In this area of worship, let us beware of simple solutions. There are those churches that feel that by adopting 'lively worship' (which can simply mean having music that is loud, long and relentlessly upbeat) they can avoid Elder Brother Syndrome and allow for free grace. Yet they need to beware of their confidence. They too face perils: it is all too easy to find that sooner or later you have to script your spontaneity, or even 'encourage' people to continue rejoicing. When you do that, the spirit of the Pharisees is not far away. There are also churches (theologically poles apart) that shun any sort of professional full-time minister, often on the grounds that he or she will restrict the freedom in worship. Yet even here it does not take very long before a rigid formality comes to dominate. Frankly, there is almost no church situation where grace cannot be driven out by ritual.

We who bear some responsibility for how churches are run must not lose sight of the central point of this parable: if God has offered his grace to people through Christ, we must not try to limit it. Negatively, if God accepts men and women freely through Jesus Christ, we must not put burdens upon them. Positively, we should stand alongside those who have become Christians, support them and rejoice with them in their new-found faith. Sourness is a nasty condition for any human to have; it is a particularly unpleasant one for those who are God's children. When newcomers to faith rejoice, try to join in with them. If you can't share their excitement, then at least walk away quietly!

We need to be realistic enough to remember that to show grace is to take a permanent risk. We need to recognise that grace is both extraordinarily messy and spectacularly elusive. It is all too often sidelined both in our individual lives and in our worship at the expense of something much tamer and more manageable. It would be lovely here to defend grace at a human level and to say that organisations that operate on grace perform better than those that work on rules and regulations. Perhaps they do. But the point about grace – the very reason why it is so risky – is quite simply that it may not work. Grace always flies in the face of justice and frequently in the face of logic and experience too. Only in the light of eternity will grace make sense. Yet we have no option: if we are in any way to imitate God, who gave himself for us in Christ, we cannot refrain from showing grace. Christians may disagree on the wisdom of portraying Christ on the cross as a religious image. Nevertheless, there is something telling about a God who stretches his arms wide in suffering, yet also in welcome.

The Big Picture

We make no apology for having looked at a lot of the details in Jesus' picture of the Prodigal. They are, after all, both interesting and helpful. Yet, as with viewing a painting, we must eventually stand back from a study of brushstrokes to take in the whole canvas. It is time to do just that.

What, in the briefest terms, is the Parable of the Prodigal all about? The answer is that it is a celebration of grace. If we define grace as 'unconditional kindness given to an undeserving recipient at an uncomfortable cost', we see that the parable illustrates all three aspects. We see in the younger son someone who is utterly undeserving. We see in the father, both in the gift of unconditional kindness and in the way he humiliates himself to bring the rebellious son back into the family, something of the uncomfortable cost of grace. These clearly show aspects of how God – Father, Son and Spirit – sacrificially pours out his love on us.

This account places three obligations upon us. We see the need to receive grace exemplified in the younger son; the need to reflect grace as shown by the father; and the need to rejoice in grace in contrast to the sourness of the elder brother.

This parable speaks to those who are in the distant land. It offers a message of promise and encouragement; it makes an appeal for them to start the journey back. It portrays a God who offers a welcome, showing grace and gentleness rather than judgement.

This parable speaks to those who find themselves in any way

wielding authority, whether at work, church or home. The parable says that God's way forward is through gentleness and restitution rather than through judgement and rebuke. It is, to use a cluster of images, to level the score sheet, to reset the clock, to wipe the slate clean. To do this, the parable suggests, will cost us something in pain or shame. If we are to be like God, we must bear that cost ourselves. Grace hurts.

This parable speaks to those who are bystanders to transactions of grace. To those who, when faced with the lost who are found through grace, find themselves tempted to adopt the scowl and clenched fist of the elder brother, it says, 'Rejoice!' We see clearly the unpleasantness into which we can slip when we stay away from fellowship with the Father and neglect to appreciate what grace is worth.

As we read – and reread – the Parable of the Prodigal, we find that we are all somewhere in it, whether as the younger son, the father or the elder son. The way we can all find ourselves here is part of the parable's genius. It is also part of its permanent challenge.

PART THREE

Handling Relationships in the Light of the Parable of the Prodigal

So far in this book we have focused on understanding all that the Parable of the Prodigal has to tell us. Yet we can – and must – go further. In the Bible, truth is never simply something confined to the brain, as if it were some sort of abstract intellectual proposition. On the contrary, truth is always applied. It is something that must be lived out. In this third section of the book we want to challenge ourselves to think how we can apply the truths in this parable to our lives, and in particular to our relationships.

We have done this in two ways. We have created a series of questions with some suggested answers based around some of the issues that arise from this parable. Following these are a number of accounts from various people who have been able to say, 'Yes, the Parable of the Prodigal means something personal to me.' We have kept them anonymous to protect both innocent and guilty, but they are true stories.

Earlier on we were cautious about the all too common definition of a parable as 'an earthly story teaching a heavenly truth'. The fact is that, although this parable deals with the spiritual world (how we relate to God), it also has many implications for what we might call the physical world (how we relate to one another). Throughout the Bible it is clear that how we relate to God affects how we relate to other people. What we worship affects how we live. Spend your time praising God for his grace and mercy, and sooner or later you will start to reflect that grace and mercy in your own life. Focus your beliefs on a God who is harsh, cruel and judgemental, and don't be surprised to find those very things characterising your own life. (This concept goes well beyond Christianity: it is no accident that some of the cruellest dictators of the twentieth century believed that the highest principle of existence was the impersonal and brutal process of evolution.) In fact, although we could try carefully to separate out what we might call the vertical aspects of a parable (those bits that relate to God) and the horizontal elements (those bits that relate to other human beings), we don't. Not only is this not easy, it is not desirable.

Quite simply, we are going to focus this section around the three characters: the Prodigal, the father and the elder brother.

THE PRODIGAL

Are you tempted to become a prodigal?

Are you looking for pastures new? Are you wondering about seizing your inheritance and heading off? Do you feel it is 'time to move on'? These are common feelings. The temptation to be a prodigal can occur in many circumstances. It might be within a marriage, within a family, or within a work environment. It can apply spiritually, for instance when someone has grown up in a Christian environment but has tired of it and wants to head over the horizon. As an aside, it is probably worth noting that in many cases, when you hear people talking about how they lost their faith and left the church, what actually happened was the reverse: they wanted to experience 'greener pastures' and so found it convenient to lose any rationale for staying inside the fence. What causes this desire to 'play the prodigal' varies. It might be because you find you are in a situation that is genuinely difficult; it might be simply because you are bored; or it might be because somehow there is an irresistible longing for something new. Whatever the ingredients, the fact is that you are getting ready to walk out and head into the distance.

Here, though, we need to pause. It is easy to fast-forward in this parable to the end without considering the pain involved. Jesus uses only a few words to describe what happened to the younger son when he left home, but what he sketches is something that, after the first mad spendthrift days, was an extended spiral downwards into misery. True, the son was ultimately restored to his father, but he suffered utter wretchedness first. And, of course, it was not just him who suffered. Although we are not directly told that the father grieved for him, it seems a certainty that this was what happened. The Prodigal's return may have ended one pain, but it began a new one and subjected the family to forces that threatened to tear it apart. Playing the prodigal can be a painful process for all concerned.

Actually, being a prodigal is not just an expensive form of learning; it is also a very inefficient one. After all, what do we see in the end? The Prodigal is back just where he started. Fairy stories often include a little phrase that tells us that the rescued character was now both 'a sadder and wiser person'. The Bible's story gives us no such reassurance. We can only hope that the younger son was indeed now wiser, but we have no such certainty.

It is also worth remembering that not only may there be much pain with little gain, there may also be wounds. Although we might wish otherwise, some actions have lasting consequences. Drink, drugs, promiscuity, squandering financial resources: all leave a legacy behind them. Yes, God can restore much of what is lost – and in his mercy often does – but there are no guarantees. Actions may be forgiven, but their legacy can live on. Even repentance cannot bring back a lost youth, repair a shattered mind, mend a broken heart or restore a diseased body. All prodigals come back with wounds and not all of them heal easily.

In short, if taking the road over the horizon looks tempting, the wisest action may be to pause and seek God's grace and power to endure your present setting.

Let us, however, add a cautionary note. Not all departures from home, family or work are wrong. There are conditions and circumstances where it would be a greater wrong to stay than to go. The most blatant of these is where there is abuse. To leave under such circumstances is not to be a prodigal. More subtle is the 'moral blackmail' situation where pressure is unfairly applied to ensure that someone stays in a situation they really ought to leave. It is quite common to hear of families where one or both parents have pressured a child to stay on at home. Well, umbilical cords have to be cut and sometimes it is essential to move on, even if uncertainty results. But these situations are very different from the 'give me my share of the inheritance' demands of the younger son in the parable.

Are you an invisible prodigal?

Say what we like about the young man in the parable, he at least made his state of mind clear. He begged for his inheritance, sold it quickly and left. Yet there are many people who lack his courage and decisiveness. They go through the motions of a life, but their heart is not in it. They stay in a relationship, remain part of a family, or stick with a job; they smile at the right time, say the right words and do the right things, but it doesn't really mean very much. Inwardly, they are in rebellion. They are present in body, but absent in mind and in spirit. Such people are, if you like, invisible or 'wannabe' prodigals. Identifying such people is not easy. The best you get is a fleeting, wistful, faraway look in their eyes as if they were dreaming of being someone else, somewhere else, doing something else. In all likelihood, there are many people who attend churches who are 'wannabe' prodigals. Fear, laziness, apathy or inertia keeps them in their place. They do nothing wrong, but most of the time they do nothing right either. If this is you, then you need to be honest. Recognise that there is something that is sadly wrong and try to identify what it is. To be constantly dissatisfied with where you are and always dreaming of something else is hardly a state that gives rise to contentment. Not only that, but it may be that one day circumstances will conspire so suddenly that what was once only a fantasy of walking out will suddenly become irresistibly attractive. If you feel that you are where you ought to be, then pray that God will show you how you may be content in that place.

Are you in the distant land?

Perhaps you know that you are indeed a prodigal. It may be that you have literally left where you ought to have stayed: a family, a relationship, a job, or your faith. Maybe in this distant land things are still going well for you. Maybe they are not. Perhaps (figuratively at least) you are already down there with the pigs, coveting the swill. Of course, it may be that the distant land you inhabit is merely symbolic; you may live in the same town or even in the same street as your former family, friends or fellowship, but you might as well be five thousand miles away. You have walked away.

To you, this parable encourages the hope of a return. If your flight has been from God, then the message of this parable is that if you turn to him he will be ready and waiting for you. God is that waiting, loving parent whose desire is to restore you back to him. And on the human level? Well, it gives no promise about any restoration here. How can it? Many returning prodigals have found the doors barred against them and have been greeted not by restoration, but by a rebuke. Yet it is worth trying: it may be that your humble and apologetic return will be greeted with a greater welcome than you had imagined.

THE FATHER

Can we prevent prodigals from running away?

Remember that, at least here, we need to put to one side the idea that because the father represents God he must be perfect. The father in this parable stands for God primarily in the area of his response to the returning son. We cannot draw firm conclusions on parenting from other areas of the parable. Nevertheless, there are some principles that we can apply, some which can be inferred from this passage and some which come from elsewhere in the Bible. Another reminder: we are here talking to all those who find themselves in the 'father' role, whether it is as a biological parent, friend, pastor or manager.

The first thing we need to reflect on is the point we made above to any would-be prodigals: having this sort of relationship breakdown is a mess. Looking at the Parable of the Prodigal, we see that no one really wins. The best we can say is that a messy rescue operation takes place which brings back the one son at the heavy price of alienating the other. A moment's thought will tell you that such episodes are best avoided in families, relationships and churches. There are cheaper ways of learning life's lessons. We need to do all we can to avoid them.

The second point is that sometimes you can make people into prodigals. So when differences emerge, it's all too easy to be rude, to make things difficult, to irritate and generally push people out. Eventually the frustration builds up so they feel they have to rebel. In such disputes you can almost hear the senior party say, 'It would be so much easier if they'd just get up and go.' While very few people ever actually say, 'Go on, just clear off!' it is a sentiment which can sometimes be clearly expressed without words.

We need to do all we can to prevent a relationship disintegrating to this point. By the time someone is packing their bags, things may already have reached the point of no return. How can we prevent such catastrophic breakdown? We could spend a lot of time on this, but we need to realise that there is much to be said for what we might call preventative maintenance in relationships. Let's list some positive guidelines.

- *Stop the trash from building up.* Foresters try to stop devastating woodland fires by spending time clearing away the flammable undergrowth. Relationships have similar principles. If we are not careful, rubbish builds up that a spark can easily ignite. Deal with small issues promptly rather than let them accumulate.

- *Work at having good times.* Rather simplistically, relationships can be viewed as bank accounts. The possibility of someone heading for the airport with a one-way ticket is always much higher when the relationship has moved into deficit. In the parable the elder son complained that his father had never given him the material for a barbecue with his friends. No doubt it was an exaggeration. Perhaps the father's response might have been, 'But you never asked!' Nevertheless, it might have been a wise move on the part of the father to throw a big party for the elder son much earlier. Make efforts to have good times, even if they are little good times.

- *Communicate!* Someone said about a situation at their work, 'The problem was, my boss was always too busy crisis-managing other people to ever spend any time discussing my work with me. Eventually, I became the crisis.' It is extraordinary how many problems can be headed off in work by a manager simply making time to sit down with his or her employees over a cup of coffee or a meal. Maybe, most of the time, nothing more serious than holidays, weather or sport is discussed. But links are built and the first hint of problems can be scented out before they become full-blown crises Such encounters are – to use our financial imagery – money deposited in the credit account. The same principle of keeping communications open applies at home between parents and children and husbands and wives. Make time to communicate even over the slightest things.

* *Practise forgiveness.* Forgiveness is that extraordinary process where we recognise a wrong done to us, realise we could make an issue over it and instead deliberately choose to do nothing about it. Do we have to add that forgiveness means forgetting? Sadly, in some cases all that 'forgiveness' really means is that the offence is in cold storage so that it can be brought out again on another occasion. It is always encouraging to hear of stories in which someone says to someone else, 'You know, you have forgiven me so much,' and gets the surprised response, 'Really? Have I?' It is a measure of someone who truly forgives that they cannot remember what they have forgiven.

Yet we need to remember again that the best solution to the problem of having a prodigal is to prevent it happening in the first place. As the saying goes, 'Prevention is better than cure.'

How are we to deal with a 'prodigal son'?

Sadly, it may be that you are able to take this question literally. A lot of parents do have sons and daughters who will decide that they need to try to make a living for themselves on their own. But of course, as we have been pointing out, the reference here is broader than children. There can be prodigals in any relationship; there are husbands, wives, business partners and even parents who turn their back on someone close to them, saying, 'Don't call me, I'll call you,' and leave with that defiant farewell slam of the door behind them.

What can we do or say? Let us make some suggestions.

- *You can make sure they know that a return is possible.* It is almost always a tragedy when someone in a relationship walks out. That tragedy becomes a disaster when any hope of a return is destroyed. In the bitterness of a walkout it is all too tempting to shout after the retreating figure something along the lines of, 'Good riddance! Drop dead! I hope I never see you again!' Tempting perhaps, but not advisable. You need to build bridges, not destroy them.
- *You can be ready to welcome them back.* Although this is not a parable with a happy ending, we must be grateful that it was the father, and not the elder brother, who met the returning son. Some people in the situation of the father literally keep the bed in the spare room made for the returning one. Others have less open strategies prepared.
- *You can learn to forgive.* 'Time is a great healer' goes the cliché – but actually it isn't true. Time is only a healer if you allow it to be. Faced with someone walking out on you, there are two possibilities. One way is to try to work at healing the wound, to seek forgiveness, to try to remember the positives and to work at minimising any thoughts of hatred and revenge. The alternative is to nurse the hatred, to incubate it, constantly to make sure that it hasn't lost any teeth. Talk to old people enough, and you will soon hear of resentments and hatreds that go back fifty years or more.

What do we do when the lost return?

The short answer is: we pour grace on them. First, we show them kindness. Second, we cut out all recriminations, analysis, self-justification and the like. All that matters is that the one who was lost is now returned. There may be a time and place for an in-depth analysis of 'what went wrong', but it is not immediate. We must also be careful that we are genuinely offering free grace and not quietly chalking up the cost so that we can expect repayment later. Genuine grace has no strings attached.

Having said that, it is probably wise counsel to remember that grace will have a cost. In the parable it is tempting to ask whether the father's disastrous confrontation with the elder son might have been avoided if he had been consulted before the return. It would not have been an unreasonable strategy for a father in this sort of situation to say (perhaps over a meal) to his elder son, 'You know, if your brother did turn up, this is what I would do.'

THE ELDER BROTHER

The elder brother is the only person in the story who has no redeeming features. Can we avoid becoming like him? The parable does not help us understand how he became what he was. But again, using some of the hints in the parable and a bit of common sense, we can make some suggestions on how we can avoid the unlovely state of sourness that he represents.

How can we prevent ourselves from becoming like the elder brother?

Two things seem striking from his brief but bitter attack on his father. The first is the clear evidence of distance between the two of them. The second is the inescapable feeling that the elder son's outburst is an expression of accumulated grievances. We may be fairly sure that these outbursts about 'slaving for you', 'never disobeying your orders' and 'yet you never gave me . . .' have not suddenly been plucked out of the air. These are accusations that have been stewing for a long time.

How can we avoid this sort of thing? In many ways, what we need to try to focus on are those things we discussed earlier when considering how to avoid producing a prodigal: the emphasis on relationships, communication and forgiveness. In the case of the parable, it seems unarguable that well before the row between them a separation already existed between the father and the elder son. This is certainly true of most rows. The explosive thunderstorm that is the breakdown of a relationship does not occur from a clear blue sky. The clouds have built up; petty grievances have been allowed to fester into angry wounds. A good relationship is like a great garden. Your first impression is of a natural and spontaneous beauty, yet a more careful examination reveals long and patient labour in weeding, planting and fertilising. Such gardens do not just happen: they require diligent work. The same goes for relationships.

One other key lesson is that we need to remember that the heart of any relationship is interaction between people. We have noted how the elder son used the language of business ('slaving', 'obeying orders') to describe his relationship with his father. This speaks volumes. Although relationships may involve contracts and agreements (think of work or even marriage), such things are no more than the packaging necessary to protect a relationship. They are not the relationship itself. Once you come to focus on what are effectively 'the contractual terms' of a relationship, you are in trouble. It is very much the child's error of mistaking the wrapping of the present for the present itself.

This rule that we need to concentrate on the personal relationships rather than the rules we have created around them applies particularly to our relationship with God. All too frequently when you meet a discouraged Christian, you find that they have become focused not on God, but on secondary matters. There is a specific danger here in church situations. Imagine, for instance, that someone becomes a Christian by accepting Jesus as their Saviour. At first they rejoice in God's grace. They marvel at the way this mighty and holy God has shown them such astonishing love and forgiveness. Their lives are full of praise and rejoicing. However, the years pass and they gradually lose some of their worst habits and acquire a quiet respectability. They forget what they were. They may even rise to some sort of responsibility in their local church. Yet as this happens slowly, quietly and without any warning, they may begin to value tidiness in worship and church matters. Neatness and even discipline become welcome. Grace, with its reckless disdain for order, becomes a disruptive and troubling feature and when it emerges there is a tendency to treat it like the outbreak of a disease rather than the descent of a blessing. Priorities slowly shift and soon new sentiments are cautiously expressed.

So there are troublesome teenagers in the community who have made many lives a misery. No one asks whether we really want them to come suddenly into church rejoicing in God's forgiveness. Wouldn't we prefer that, somehow, the law dealt with them in justice? And the neighbourhood binge drinkers? Surely, it's preferable that the social services sort them out? What about those overzealous worshippers who want to stand up and spontaneously praise God when we have to finish the service at 12 o'clock? Wouldn't they be happier in another fellowship? Can you see how gradually and insidiously the spirit of the elder brother can seep even into a church?

Ultimately, we have to keep reminding ourselves of the spectacular and awesome nature of God's grace in Christ. If we realise that we ourselves are sinners who have been forgiven by grace, then we will not easily take issue when grace is shown liberally to others.

CONCLUSION

In this section we have given some advice on relationships. We hope this is helpful. Yet there is a danger with such advice that it comes over as pure, unadulterated morality. If we're not careful, we go away feeling more troubled than when we started. And it would be a pity to end the treatment of this parable on such a note. After all, this story of the Prodigal is not a parable about how to achieve success. It is a story about how to be rescued from failure. This is something we desperately need to understand. In the area of relationships, whether with God or with each other, we are all failures. We are all, to a greater or lesser extent, prodigals. All of us have rebelled not just once, but repeatedly. If we look at ourselves with anything approaching honesty, we see that we have failed to meet God's standard.

How, then, can we come to a God who is holy? The answer is that we can only come to him in humility, repentance and faith and fall at his feet. And as we look up to him, we see his arms stretched wide in welcome. Those outstretched arms do not just greet us, but they remind us that through Jesus' own suffering on the cross the price has been paid by God himself. Forgiveness can now be offered to all. However far away we have been, however distant the land we have travelled in, however deep the despair we have endured, we can be restored and embraced back into God's family.

We must learn to show the father's love to others and to avoid the cold sourness of the elder brother. This side of the grave and heaven, we will never leave the Parable of the Prodigal.

Personal Accounts

H'S ACCOUNT

Can I identify with the Parable of the Prodigal? You bet.

I was brought up in a Christian home, with a fantastic dad. But at sixteen I wanted out. I don't know why, but the fact is, I hated authority and being told what to do. I suppose I also hated the fact that my sisters were what I called 'Super-Christians'. Although I felt that I had given my life to God, I didn't seem to be able to live like them. Because I wasn't a Christian like them, I felt like the black sheep. So I walked out with nothing, just my stupid self.

I moved in with my boyfriend and had a great time for a couple of years. Then one day he left for a job. He never came back. Homeless and broke, covered in eczema and with bronchitis, I had no choice but to go home. This was the first time I had to do this: it wasn't to be the last. I rang my dad and cried down the phone. He picked me up, brought me home and cuddled me for ages. He and Mum ran a Christian guesthouse, so they gave me one of the rooms and nursed me back to health. It took a full summer.

Had I learned my lesson? No. When I was well, I began going out with boys again. The very first night after I left my parents' care I bumped into a guy. We started a relationship. Eventually he became my husband and then the father to my four girls. He was the typical know-it-all wise guy, but I loved him. My parents weren't keen on him and my father made no secret of the fact that he thought I was a fool to ruin my life on such a man. I didn't listen to him: my wilful, wild spirit didn't take kindly to advice. My dad was hurt because he loved me so much and he could see what I couldn't, that my relationship was going to be a disaster. Do I need to say that my father was right? One morning, my husband left to move in with his new soulmate. To this very day I have never seen or heard from him.

A year later I found myself in a really black place. Thinking about it all now, I believe that my love for my husband was so great that he had somehow come between God and me. It wasn't until he was removed from my life that I could see my real heavenly Father. In the depths of despair, I found myself praying to God. I began to pray and stopped. 'God, I guess I've hurt you and too many people for you to forgive me. I get that, but I am truly sorry.' I only found out later that, at the exact time I was praying this, my dad was on his knees begging for Christ to intervene and save my soul.

I came to a genuine faith in Christ shortly afterwards. Yet I still had a long journey! I had some huge apologies to make. One very sad time was when I thought that the relationship between my dad and me was over. I couldn't bring myself to face him. I went to a phone box, not really knowing what to expect, and called him. I started crying, begging him to forgive me. He just said, 'I love you, your dinner's on the table.'

I wish I could say that my sisters welcomed me back. In fact, when I declared that I had become a child of God, their reaction was shock and anger. I could sense them wondering: how could God pick me? They knew that I just wasn't good enough. I felt that they were watching me closely, waiting for me to slip, but God in his mercy protected me and my little girls. I plodded on. I tried to make a home with Christ as the head. I threw myself into church activities. I couldn't get enough of reading the Bible, yet I knew that with my sisters I never really counted for much.

Today I count myself very blessed. I know my Lord forgives me and I love him, but actions have a price and I have paid for my wildness. I can't turn the clock back; the wounds have healed, but I still have the scars. Both my sisters continue to have major issues with the amount of time that my parents spent on sorting out my life. One believes that the amount of time Mum and Dad spent with my children meant her children were neglected, so they have very little to do with our parents. I guess they won me back, but it cost them a lot.

Can I identify with the Parable of the Prodigal? Oh yes.

G'S ACCOUNT

I had a close encounter with Christianity at the age of nineteen when I went with some friends from music college to a Billy Graham rally. It was a powerful and emotional event and at the end there was an invitation for people to come to the front to give their lives to Christ. I rose to my feet and was about to step forward when I suddenly had the overwhelming feeling that this was mass hypnotism. I sat down and refused to go forward. And that, for the time being, was that. As I look back on that evening when I rejected God's gracious offer of love through Jesus, I see myself as the Prodigal Son, turning his face away from his father and striding off into the distance.

For years afterwards I gave Christianity very little thought. Indeed, I chose to go my own way and soon found myself leading a pretty self-centred and unwholesome lifestyle. I toured the country with an orchestra, never staying in one place for more than two weeks at a time, living the 'high life'. I found myself always looking for love, but never finding it.

Marriage and two sons followed, but not happiness. Soon I was struck by a serious nervous breakdown and slid into a dark depression, which made life awful not just for me, but also for my family. Then followed ten years of pills and despair; during that time I began to look desperately for a way out of the pit of misery into which my life had descended.

I now see that although I had rejected God during these wilderness years, he had never given up on me. I feel that the instant I started to turn back to God, like the father in the parable, he was there waiting. My mother-in-law, who had been praying for me since I married, gave me Michael Green's book *You Must Be Joking*. As I read it, I knew that there just had to be more to life than what I had experienced so far. At the end of the book, I found my answer . . . Jesus. I prayed the prayer Michael Green suggested and there, in the quiet of my home, gave God my life. I have never looked back!

Since coming to know the father's patient love for a prodigal, I've come to understand – this time from the perspective of the other side – those who are in a 'prodigal position'. In my current church I have become co-leader of two amazing monthly outreach events, Prayer Café and Prayer Stop. There are over fifty of us and we go out to invite people in off the street. Many of the stories that we hear from our guests are often utterly heartbreaking. Frequently the difficulties they suffer stem from broken family relationships, loneliness, drug and alcohol abuse and deprivation of all kinds. In the case of those who 'live on the street', it is often a combination of these factors. In the course of this work we encounter every race, colour and creed and do our best to ensure that all are made welcome. We make it our principle to love these people as Jesus does and try to show them that there is a safe place where they will be listened to, prayed with (if requested), fed and refreshed in every sense.

Having once been a prodigal, I suppose I now identify with the father. I find myself filled with longing to bring the destitute, lonely and hurting into a place where the 'feast' is not just home-made cakes, but also God's love made real. Our welcome stems from a genuine God-given desire to bring love, comfort and rest to all the people who come in. Regardless of what has happened in their lives in the past, and what they are now, we long for them to know that they are accepted by us just as God accepts them in Christ.

P'S ACCOUNT

I'm seventy now and can honestly say that after many struggles I have come to know something of what it means to show the spirit of forgiveness that is at the heart of the Parable of the Prodigal.

I gave my life to Christ sixty years ago when I was a young girl of ten. I was being sexually abused at the time and I had hoped that the 'loving' God to whom I had given my life would stop what was going on. When the abuse continued, I became confused. A couple of years later my family moved to another country, but sexual abuse began again with totally different people. By now I had become totally disillusioned with God. I survived the abuse and ended up marrying a wonderful man. Over the next twenty or so years, we had three beautiful children. If you had asked me, I would have said that I was reasonably happy with my lot, but deeper down I was gradually beginning to realise that something was missing from my life. I began searching in all the wrong places for something or someone to fill the emptiness I felt deep inside. Deep down, the effects of the sexual abuse were still festering and they spilled over not just into my life, but also into the life of my family.

When my daughter was thirteen, she became a Christian and began to pray for me. Five years later I was confirmed in the Anglican Church. Although over the years I had rebelled against God, when I turned back to him he showed me overwhelming goodness and grace. Nevertheless, the next few years were hard.

The Lord began to lead me through a wilderness experience which lasted for about ten years and then gradually he began to open up healing to me over the sexual abuse I had suffered.

The fact is that, deep down, I really hadn't forgiven those who had abused me years earlier. Gradually God forced me into learning about forgiveness. I bitterly opposed this. Nothing in me wanted to forgive and everything in me cried out, 'I wasn't at fault and I shouldn't need to forgive! I was one of the victims!' On one occasion, after reading an article that suggested writing a letter to an abuser, spelling out the effects of the abuse, then burning the letter, I wrote fourteen letters! As I knelt by the fireplace with a match in my hand, I suddenly heard God speaking clearly in my heart: 'Now forgive them!'

The impact of God's words was physical. I can still remember feeling as winded as if someone had punched me in the stomach. 'How could you, God?' I cried in unbelief. 'How could you expect me to forgive them for all the pain of a lifetime? Pain that brought suffering not only to me, but also to my husband and children! How could I ever forgive them?'

God reminded me of a previous incident of forgiveness in my workplace and I was suddenly aware that I could do it – with God's help. Trusting that God would put the forgiveness I needed in my heart, I proceeded to forgive each offender in turn. When I had forgiven the last one, I set fire to the letters and, as the flames rose, the peace that fell on me was like a warm, heavy blanket.

I would have been happy to let the matter end there, but it was not to be. God had other plans. I spent twenty-five years of my working life in a police environment and, as you can imagine, had acquired something of a tough attitude towards criminals – particularly sexual offenders. When I retired from work, I became part of a prayer team to support the first Alpha course to be held in a prison in this country. Prayer I could handle. However, it was not long before I was asked by one of the team to go out to the prison to meet the men for whom I had been praying. I declined. The other two members of the prayer team accepted the invitation. As they carried on going each week, they tried to talk me into going with them. Eventually their persistence won me over and I gave in and said, 'OK, just this once.'

From that first time, I carried on with a prison ministry team for the next six years and did Alpha courses, Bible studies and a monthly church service. Then came the day I had always feared would come. I was asked by the chaplain to be part of an Alpha team in the sexual abuse wing. I really didn't want to do it, but I knew God wanted me to. I knew he wanted me to show his fatherly love to these people.

On the first day of that Alpha course we were given a very small room. There were six team members and seventeen men in this small room. We were so densely packed that we were in effect right in each other's faces! One of the prisoners followed me around, talking to me and trying to look me in the face, but I could not make eye contact with him. All I had suffered came back to me and I felt I was in the presence of a monster. Then, suddenly, I was able to look into his eyes and found to my extraordinary surprise that he was simply a man. From then on we began to do church in this wing also. One Sunday, it was my turn to do the talk and the leader – who knew something of my past experiences – asked if I would give Communion after my talk. I have to say that this was the most moving thing I had ever done in my life. I felt strangely aware that the Lord had prepared me over so many years to come face to face with these men who had committed offences just like the ones that had so devastated my life. It was God who had helped me to see these men no longer as monsters, but as broken people who, out of their own pain, had hurt other people. It was an awesome experience. I have learned that God shows the father's love to us, so that we might show it to others.

M'S ACCOUNT

My family lived on the island of Lewis. I was the practical male in the family. Whenever there was work to be done, I would be at my father's side learning how to do the tasks. My sister and brother were the academic ones, while I was set on a life on the island. Nevertheless, I was not entirely content. I found myself distinctly jealous of my younger brother when he went onto the mainland to further his education. I remember telling my mother that I felt I was meant to do something, but I did not know what it was.

In 1985 we moved into another house on Lewis, one next to a Church of Scotland manse. As a result, my father felt it would be appropriate for us to attend church. I went to church for around six months simply because I was told to, but I soon began to realise uncomfortably that my relationship with the God they were talking about was not right. I knew about him, but did not know him. I began to feel that God was starting to speak to me, using his people to let me know he was calling me. I found this quite daunting and I felt that I was not what he was looking for.

On Remembrance Sunday, 11 November 1985, the minister was directing our thoughts to the sacrifices made for us in past generations. He said that although it was important to remember these, it was even more important to remember the love God showed us in the sacrifice of his Son. He then went on to discuss the Parable of the Prodigal Son and highlighted the love the father had for the son who was lost. As he talked about the relationship between the eldest son and the father, I began to see the similarity I had to that son. I was the son who stayed at home and helped my mum and dad around the house. I began to see my desperate need for God in my life. I realised that God had been speaking to me and that this could be the last time he would call.

After the service I was sitting with my family at Sunday lunch when I was gripped with conviction. I looked at my family through a glaze of tears, knowing I needed Christ. My body began to convulse and at the dinner table I felt the love of Christ wash over me. I knew that Christ had entered my heart. I now think that I was both the prodigal son and the elder son.

After that, I worked in my local church for five years, becoming a deacon and Sunday school teacher. I left the island in 1990 to try to get into the care sector, but I was not educated enough. I had the dream that I wanted to make a difference. I applied to the local technical college, but given my lack of academic background, I was not very confident about how I would get on. Nevertheless, the Lord was faithful: six years later I emerged with a degree in primary teaching. The Lord led me onwards and my heart began to go out to the vulnerable in our society and I started to work with disabled children and adults. After further qualifications, I went on to get a training job in one of the largest universities in Scotland. I now run my own learning centre.

Now married and a father of two boys, I am the Sunday school superintendent in a small church in a very difficult area of Aberdeen. We reach out to people whose Christian heritage is amazing, but the toils of life have left their scars. After having been both the younger and the elder son, I am now the father in the parable who longs to see the lost return home.

L'S ACCOUNT

I grew up in a strict Christian home in South Africa and had to go to Sunday school until I was eighteen. I was a good and well-behaved kid. One problem I had with Christianity was this: I always thought to myself, 'How can you actually love God or anyone you have never met?' Although we proclaimed our love for God each Sunday in church, this question remained with me because I didn't feel any real kind of 'physical' love for God. Nevertheless, I knew I ought to love him and most of the time I felt I did.

When I was twenty and at university, I had my first kiss from a boy. That, of course, raised lots of questions: how far can you go with a boy before it is a sin? Suddenly I realised that neither my church nor any books could – or would – give me an answer. Linked to that came another thought: perhaps my religion is just a scare and there isn't a devil who will strike you with his fork. And with that, my rebellion started.

Soon it wasn't just the boyfriend; I started to drink and smoke, and began to party seven days a week. Coming to the UK to study seemed to free me even further from my conservative church and cultural background. When I turned twenty-one, I received the proceeds of a life policy that an aunt had taken out when I was a baby. What did I do with it? I drank the lot. For years, I lived a godless life and did some horrible things. I even had an abortion and suffered years of guilt as a result. I realised that my life had little meaning and, partly to continue my rebellion against my background and partly to try to find answers to life, I now tried every religion out there. As the years went by, I got more depressed and this only increased when, at the age of twenty-seven, I broke up with the boyfriend I had wanted to marry. I could see my life as a black tunnel gradually closing in on me. Circumstances got worse. I was in the UK on my last student visa and was forced to return to South Africa without money and without a future.

One day, out of the blue, my greatest enemy, the girlfriend of my ex-boyfriend, phoned and asked if she could see me. I agreed largely because I wanted to know how things were between her and the ex, as I hadn't had contact with either for three years. So we met up and I was surprised to find that she spoke about God all the time. She told me that she'd had a dream about me and that she knew I was carrying the whole world on my shoulders and it was too heavy. What was weird was that the whole time she was talking I felt as if someone was stabbing big holes in my body and I could almost physically feel how the dark deadness seemed to flow out from me.

She invited me to come to their Bible meeting on a Saturday. I agreed, but again for wrong motives; I wanted to see my ex again and to find out more about their situation. When I arrived, actually I wasn't really in the mood, because I wanted to go and watch the rugby in the pub and get drunk as usual – but, as they say, curiosity killed the cat. There was a guy who gave the talk, and in my mind I was fighting everything he said. I kept on saying in my mind, 'I've heard all about it before. I've been brought up with all that, but it doesn't work. Where is this power? I have never actually seen it.'

Despite my scepticism, I came back the following week and this time, before they started the talk, my ex's girlfriend said that we should sing a song. I thought I was going to die of embarrassment and desperately wished I had gone to the pub instead. I mean, who sings on a Saturday afternoon in a little group at home while there's a big rugby game on? Then, as soon as the music started, I felt the tears coming and for the life of me I couldn't stop them. Weirdly, though, I really didn't feel sad. I was embarrassed, and I really hoped that the earth would open up and swallow me. So there I was, crying my eyes out, and as the tears fell down my face I saw this incredible light with a person in the middle. As I saw this person, I literally felt all the depression and darkness leave my body. It was the most extraordinary, the most supernatural, thing I have ever experienced. The change and newness that I felt were so overwhelming that I had to open my eyes slightly to check to see if I was still wearing my clothes, because I felt so terribly different!

For the rest of the meeting, I didn't say a word and at the end they gave me a wristband with the letters WWJD (What Would Jesus Do) on it. I put it on my wrist and I was extremely self-conscious about it, but I felt as if I belonged to some awesome group. I walked home that night and felt as light as a feather. For the whole of that first week, I kept looking in the mirror several times a day, because the difference felt so physical and severe. I even opened my cupboard a few times to see if perhaps I had bought a whole new wardrobe and had just forgotten about it, but no, the face and the clothes were the same. It was all on the inside and spiritual. I really knew then what the Bible meant by the old person dying and you becoming new. In fact, the whole Bible seemed to come alive.

At the time I was still living with my boyfriend. After a week, he just burst out and said that he didn't know what had happened to me; he felt there was a complete stranger in his house. That was a fantastic testimony to me. However, I realised that things had to change and that I needed to move out and find my own place.

From then on, everything changed. God restored my life. I found a Christian husband soon after that and he even had a visa for the UK. The depression miraculously vanished. I've been through very tough times since, but I've never been depressed. We have now been married for seven years and have three gorgeous children. I came from nothing in the gutter and now I have all this, and I have God as my Father who forgave me all my evil and destructive past. The story of the Prodigal is the story of my life.

R'S ACCOUNT

I am a minister of a church. Sadly, I have to say that I have seen some members of my church behave like the older brother in Jesus' story.

For the last five years I have been working in an area with a high percentage of refugees and asylum seekers. Over the years several have attended worship regularly and have tried to make their home with us. It pains me to say that many of them have met prejudice and racism from some members of the congregation, especially when we have tried to embrace new ways of worshipping which reflect the world Church. The sour and dismissive comments I have received on various occasions are as follows: 'You love them more than us. What about us? We are the ones who have built this church and have kept it going. Don't we matter any more?' Or, even worse, 'They are taking over; it does not feel like it's my church any more.'

I could go on, but I hope this gives a flavour of the 'elder brother hang-ups' that still prevail. As a minister I often feel like the father as I love them all, but my heart breaks when I experience these hurtful comments, as they have completely failed to understand God's grace and cannot bring themselves to rejoice with those who do.

E'S ACCOUNT

When Christians talk about how they came to faith, a lot of what they say follows a similar pattern. They talk of how they were in deep trouble, often stuck in some spectacular sin, and then how, one day, they cried out to God or Jesus for mercy. From that day – sometimes a specific moment – their life turned around. As I grew up, I heard many such testimonies and for many years I really struggled listening to them, because it didn't happen that way for me. I didn't remember my conversion, didn't have some amazing revelation and didn't suddenly have my darkness lifted by God's light. And that became the problem.

I was raised in a Christian home and it seems that from the moment of my birth I went to church. My parents were Christians and prayed for me and taught me God's word. I went to Sunday school and, later, Christian camps during the holidays. As long as I can remember, God was a part of my life. Nevertheless, my knowledge of God did deepen as, over time, I gradually got to know him better and in a more personal manner. One way this happened was that God brought certain people into my life. For instance, when I went to high school, I became good friends with a girl who was really enthusiastic about God, really didn't care what other people thought about her and just went 'all out' for Jesus. That level of commitment and enthusiasm was a real revelation for me. I think it is fair to say that until then, my God was effectively my parents' God. From then on, though, he became much more my God. Soon after entering my teens I began to feel that in some way Jesus was big enough in my heart for me to declare it. So I got baptised. At more or less the same time, I began to read the Bible and pray on a daily basis. In my own quiet way I felt God's presence with me and almost every time I prayed I felt he spoke to me. All was well.

Yet as I continued through my teenage years and I heard other people's dramatic stories of how they had become Christians, I began to feel that something was missing. Particularly at church, I was constantly exposed to people who had experienced this moment of conversion when they had accepted Christ into their heart. Their entry into the Christian life had been spectacular: they had left their lives of sin and every aspect of their personality had been transformed. When such people spoke in church – they 'gave their testimony' – they would confidently use phrases like 'I'm sure everyone remembers the first time they received Jesus', and I would see everybody about me nod in solemn agreement. Sometimes they would say how, immediately after their conversion, their friends and relatives had all seen something different in them. And again, there would be nods and murmurs of understanding from the congregation.

They didn't come from me. Quite simply, I really couldn't identify with what they were talking about. In fact, I began to long for what they had experienced. I almost wanted deliberately to go away from God, just so that I could have a big 'Wow!' story to tell of how Jesus saved me from a terrible life. It may well be that, subconsciously or even consciously, I actually wanted to experience some of those tantalising sins these people had now so definitely and miraculously put behind them. It all seemed astonishingly unfair. They had experienced much more of God's forgiveness than I had! I felt I had lost out. They were superstars, almost celebrities, and I was an overlooked nothing. No one ever asked me for my testimony, because I didn't have one. The absence of this astonishing and miraculous action of grace in my life had made me feel like a second-class citizen.

Eventually, I grew out of this. I saw my desire to sin so that I might know forgiveness as perverse stupidity. I came to realise that I was no less a Christian than those who had gone through spectacular conversions. With age (and, hopefully, wisdom), I have now come to be profoundly grateful both for the stable and supportive upbringing that God gave me and for the way that I came to know him at a very early age.

How does this relate to the Parable of the Prodigal? Quite simply, it is because I can relate to the elder brother. As a teenager I was frankly bitter that while these other people were out there enjoying themselves, wallowing in sin, I was sitting quietly at home honouring my mother and father and serving God. I felt that my decision to follow God dutifully should have been rewarded; yet it wasn't. In fact, their rebellion seemed more praised than my righteousness. I was both judgemental and jealous. I was blessed by God, was loved and protected by him, and yet I could only see the status of other people.

Later, God showed me that my attitude was itself sin. It was not just the fact that I was jealous of the experiences of others and happy to stand in judgement over them; it was the fact that I saw myself as innocent and without sin. The reality was that I was nothing of the sort. Although my sins might not have been public or spectacular, they were still sins. I came to see that I needed to know Christ, to receive his forgiveness. Indeed, I still do. But I realise that it is easy to be an elder brother.

Appendix:
The Use and Abuse of
Parables Today

This is intended to be a practical book, and a very practical question is this: To what extent in Christian teaching do we use parables today?

Some people have argued that we should actually back off from what is called propositional teaching to a more parabolic or narrative style of teaching. They say we should shift from predominantly declaring truth to sharing stories. Indeed, some people go further and talk about story or narrative being at the heart of sharing the Christian faith. For them, becoming a Christian is not so much about subscribing to a set of truths, but more about identifying in some way with a story.

Let's consider this carefully. It should be obvious that neither of us has got anything against the parables or stories. We would hardly write this book with its extensive elaboration of the tale of the Prodigal unless we felt that story was important. (Indeed, Chris writes fiction for a hobby.) We believe that there is much in favour of parables and long to see more new stories for our generation. In a sound-bite world, unfamiliar with perhaps forty minutes of discussing factual or propositional statements ('*this* is true; *that* isn't'), stories have an appeal and charm. The merits of parables that we have already mentioned are considerable: their flexibility, the way they invite both reflection and involvement, and the way they get around barriers.

And yet. There are several problems with narrative or parabolic preaching that need considering. The first is that parables aren't as easy as you think. Like a good recipe, they are easily spoiled by both omissions and additions. So you could write a story, only to find that everybody becomes fascinated by a minor figure who has no significance whatsoever. Second, the elusive aspect of parables (their *if-the-cap-fits-wear-it* character) can cause problems. Yes, it can mean that people suddenly recognise their own sins and failings in the story, but it can also allow them to worm their way out of the issues raised. 'After all,' they can say, 'it was only a story.'

The third and most serious problem, though, is the fact that you cannot really make a belief system out of parables. So, for instance, all the historic denominations of Christianity hold to what are called confessions of faith. One of the oldest examples of this is called the Apostles' Creed, which opens with the line, 'I believe in God the Father.' It's a blunt, unequivocal statement that you either agree with or don't agree with. In fact, if parables are written to allow ambiguity, creeds are written to exclude it. You can't build anything like a creed out of parables; they are very different. This is why, in our discussion of what this parable means, we have been very careful to buttress our conclusions with statements from the 'non-parable elements' of the Bible such as the New Testament letters. The very flexibility and slippery fluidity that allows parables to slide through defences means that they cannot become solid and unyielding building blocks of faith. And, as we have noted before, in the sense that Jesus used parables, the early church avoided them. From the giving of the Spirit on the day of Pentecost, the main method of preaching and teaching has been to declare statements of truth.

This is not to dismiss parables entirely. In the form of extended illustrations they may be an excellent introduction or addition to propositional teaching. But they cannot replace it. Perhaps the most useful place for parables, especially in those parts of the Western world that are becoming aggressively anti-Christian, is in the preaching of the good news outside the Church. If, as seems to be the trend, Christianity moves from being marginalised to being actively persecuted in the West, we may once again need to resort to parables. Parables can be effective where sermons are silenced.

Notes

PART TWO

INTRODUCTION

1 This is a widely quoted statement, but it has proved hard to locate exactly where the great author said it.

CHAPTER 1

1 Leviticus 25:23.

CHAPTER 2

1 Acts 16 starts in the third person and changes to 'we' in verse 11. See also Colossians 4:14; 2 Timothy 4:11; Philemon 24.
2 e.g. Luke 21:20–8.
3 Klyne Snodgrass, *Stories with Intent* (Eerdmans, 2008), p. 24: 'For all intents and purposes, the early church did not tell parables.' And, 'After the resurrection of Jesus the parabolic mode, which is a prophetic mode, appears to have been dropped in favour of more direct avenues of gospel proclamation.'

CHAPTER 3

1 The best examples are 2 Samuel 12:1–14; 14:1–20; 1 Kings 20:35–42; Isaiah 5:1–7.

2 Mark 4:32–4.

3 The Greek word *parabole* has a much broader meaning in the Gospels than the English word *parable*. For parables as stories, see Luke 15:11–32; 18:1–8; as proverbs, Mark 3:24–5; Luke 4:23; as similes and metaphors, Matthew 5:14; 10:16; as riddles Mark 7:15; 14:58; as comparisons, Matthew 13:33; Luke 15:3–7; as examples, Luke 10:30–35; 12:16–21; or even as allegories, Mark 4:3–9; 12:1–12.

4 Snodgrass, *Stories with Intent*, p. 9.

5 C. S. Lewis, 'On Science Fiction', in *Essay Collection and other Short Pieces* (HarperCollins, 2000), p. 454.

6 Mark 1:43–5; 3:7–9.

7 Matthew 7:28–9; Mark 1:27; John 6:68; 7:45–6.

8 For example, Matthew 21:28; Luke 11:5.

9 Mark 4:10–12.

10 Mark 4:33–4.

11 Matthew 13:1–23; Mark 4:1–20; Luke 8:1–15.

CHAPTER 4

1 The quoted passage is from Nehemiah 9:17. Virtually identical passages are to be found in Numbers 14:18; Psalms 86:15; 103:8; 145:8; Joel 2:13; Jonah 4:2; Nahum 1:3.

2 John 8:7.

3 Isaiah 40:11; see also Ezekiel 34:11–16.

4 John 10:1–21.

CHAPTER 5

1 Deuteronomy 21:17.
2 Deuteronomy 5:16.
3 Luke 18:1–7.
4 Luke 16:1–9.
5 Matthew 5:22, 28.

CHAPTER 7

1 Matthew 21:28–32.
2 Matthew 25:14–30.
3 Matthew 25:24–5.
4 Matthew 5:21–2; 23:23; Luke 11:42.
5 Luke 10:25–8.
6 Matthew 7:7–11; 21:22.

CHAPTER 8

1 Romans 6:23.
2 Galatians 3:10, 13; also 2 Corinthians 5:21.
3 Romans 3:22–6.
4 1 Peter 3:18.
5 Isaiah 53:3–12; 1 Peter 2:24.
6 John 3:16.
7 Matthew 5:7; 6:12 (Today's NIV uses 'debts' and 'debtors' here).
8 See Revelation 3:17.

Selected Books
for Further Reading

On parables generally
Craig Blomberg, *Interpreting the Parables* (IVP, 1990).
Kyle Snodgrass, *Stories with Intent: A comprehensive guide to the parables of Jesus* (Eerdmans, 2008).

On the Parable of the Prodigal
K. E. Bailey, *Finding the Lost: Cultural Keys to Luke 15* (Concordia, 1992).
K. E. Bailey, *The Cross and the Prodigal: Luke 15 through the eyes of Middle Eastern Peasants*, 2nd edn (IVP, 2005).

On Luke's Gospel
Joel Green, *The Gospel of Luke*. The New International Commentary on the New Testament (Eerdmans, 1978).
J.John and Chris Walley, *The Life: A Portrait of Jesus* (Authentic, 2004).
I. Howard Marshall, *The Gospel of Luke: A Commentary on the Greek Text*. NIGTC (Eerdmans, 1978).
John Nolland, *Luke*, Word Biblical Commentaries, 3 vols (Paternoster Press, 1989–1993).